THE LITTLE GIRL
ON THE ICE FLOE

Adélaïde Bon

THE LITTLE GIRL ON THE ICE FLOE

*Translated from the French
by Tina Kover*

Europa
editions

Europa Editions
214 West 29th Street
New York, N.Y. 10001
www.europaeditions.com
info@europaeditions.com

Copyright © Éditions Grasset & Fasquelle, 2018
First Publication 2019 by Europa Editions

Translation by Tina Kover
Original title: *La petite fille sur la banquise*
Translation copyright © 2019 by Europa Editions

Library of Congress Cataloging in Publication Data is available
ISBN 978-1-60945-515-6

Bon, Adélaïde
The Little Girl on the Ice Floe

Book design and cover illustration by Emanuele Ragnisco
www.mekkanografici.com

Prepress by Grafica Punto Print – Rome

Printed in the USA

CONTENTS

To Doctor Muriel Salmona,
to the tireless investigator,
to all the victims of violence,
my heroines.

When crimes begin to accumulate,
they become invisible. When suffering
becomes unbearable, no one hears the cries
anymore. The screams fall like summer rain.
—BERTOLT BRECHT

THE LITTLE GIRL
ON THE ICE FLOE

D id she wipe her mouth with the back of her hand, run her tongue over her teeth, fix her hair a bit? Did she pull up her underpants, straighten her pinafore, tug the white blouse back down—or did he? She watches him, chin bobbing like one of those little nodding dogs on the rear parcel shelf of a car. *I'm a nice girl. I'm pretty. I like it. You're my friend. You like big thighs. You're good to me. I am a gourmand. I won't say anything. It's our secret, I promise. I won't say a thing.* Words he's said to her that she doesn't remember, any more than she remembers what he's done to her.

She picks up the white paper bag of sweets and the tin of goldfish flakes she'd put down on the corner of a step.

Something has tilted; she's not sure if it's herself or the floor. She concentrates on climbing the stairs.

She turns around on the landing when he calls her, promising again, nodding her head.

She's lying on her bed, trying to catch a tear on the tip of her tongue. The floorboards creak in the corridor. She picks up her book. *Nobody's Boy*, by Hector Malot.

"Is your book making you cry?" asks her father—concerned, perhaps, because she slipped like a shadow from the apartment's foyer to her room without the usual thunderous shout of *Hello, dear family of mine*, without slamming the front door, without coming to tell them about her day.

Her head moves. Left. Right. Right. Left.

"Did something happen?"
Her head moves. Up. Down. Down. Up.

She's sitting between her parents on the wine-colored living room sofa. Her brother and sisters have disappeared. She stares at the wallpaper as if she doesn't recognize it, like she doesn't recognize her own parents. Everything has changed, suddenly, and she can't understand why. They're talking to her, but she can't quite hear them or understand them. She's floating.

She's sitting next to her father in the back seat of a police car. The police officers are turning on the revolving lights to make her smile. She smiles. She's a nice girl. She's no longer there. She's dead, only no one seems to realize it.

At the police station, a woman officer asks her questions. She has to answer "yes" or "no." She nods or shakes her head, depending on the answer. She doesn't feel anything. The woman police officer writes: *He touched me down there, in the front and the back. He grabbed my left hand and put it on his penis.*

They tell her she's lodging a complaint for *sexual touching* and that the man from the stairwell is a *pedophile.* She nods.

She can't feel the jellyfish twisting inside her on that day; she can't feel the long, transparent tentacles penetrating her. She doesn't know that their filaments are going to drag her, little by little, into a story that isn't her own, that doesn't concern her. She doesn't know that they're going to derail her completely, pull her down to solitary and unwelcoming depths, hobble her every step, make her doubt her own strength, shrink the world around her year by year until it's nothing but a tiny air pocket with no way out. She doesn't know that she is at war now, or that the enemy forces are inside her.

No one warns her. No one explains. The world has gone quiet.

The years will pass. They'll forget about this sunny Sunday in May—or they won't talk about it, at least. She won't think about it anymore, either.

You'd had arguments and heartache before that, too, of course. Angry times and defeats and funerals. You'd already learned that loving someone very much doesn't stop them from dying, but that you can still talk to them afterward, the way you used to talk to Grandpa under the plum tree. You knew there were illnesses that couldn't be cured, and questions that couldn't be answered—and yet you knew, too, that the glittering, dewy spiderwebs held answers that could never be put into words. God lived in the deepest, warmest part of your heart, and in the humming of insects in the springtime. You climbed to the very tops of the trees, to feel yourself sway with them in the breeze. You had a boyfriend who fenced, for whom you drew sketches of the twelve children you'd have together someday. You threw tantrums, flinging yourself down on the pavement and flatly refusing to get up. You collected pretty words, keeping lists of them in notebooks, and lists of crazy words, too. You wanted to be a firefighter, to save the world, to be a great writer. You didn't give a damn about mirrors or appearances. You were nine years old.

I

S he tells her boyfriend about it the next day. Lunch break is over, and they're standing beside his desk. I can't remember how she said it, exactly, which words she used, but she felt like something had shifted, and she owed it to herself to tell him. She doesn't wait for his response, but goes and sits down, her back very straight.

She starts eating more. She always liked to eat before, too. I don't know if she realizes that she isn't eating to nourish herself anymore, but to comfort herself.

She has everything a person needs to be happy. Her childhood is privileged, sheltered. She's healthy, pretty, intelligent. She lives in Paris, goes skiing in the winter and swimming in the summer, visits museums abroad. She comes from a good family in a nice neighborhood; she's been well brought up, she knows how to behave in polite society. She's white, with French roots going all the way back to Charlemagne and to Morvan I, king of the Bretons. She was raised in the Catholic Church, brought up to care for others, and one of her grandfathers gave his life in the service of France. Her father is successful, and so is her mother. Both of her parents are industrious, they love their jobs, they work in high value-added industries; their lives are active, abundant, fertile. They're busy, clumsy, tender parents, and deeply loving ones.

When she's alone, she talks to an enormous white yeti that only she can see, and to Pandi Panda, her old stuffed bear. They protect her; they make her feel safe, and she can tell them anything. She still sucks her thumb. She often holds the yeti's hand when they're out in the street, or when there are too many people around, when she can't manage to keep an eye on everything all by herself.

Some days, the things around her talk to each other, and she can spend a whole hour in the bathroom, not moving, listening to their conversations in her head.

Some nights, in the years that follow, right when she's in the middle of a dream, something interrupts the story—something, a specific spot she notices on her body that starts turning, faster and faster, and the whirlwind gets bigger and sucks her in, and the edges of her body start to crumble away, little by little—but she can't look away; her body is a desert, shifting and dissolving; the sand is viscous, and it pours into her mouth. There's nothing to hold on to, and she slips and slides and melts, and when the whirlwind has filled up the whole space of the dream, when she's just about to disappear, she screams. She wakes up with a start, and she listens. She's afraid of actually having screamed, of having woken her parents. There's something horribly dirty about the dream, something she must never tell.

The following spring, she is ten years old, and gets a white hoodie. She's happy to wear something other than crew necks and smocked dresses, for once. One of the coolest, most popular girls on the playground compliments her outfit, and her heart overflows—she, who feels so worthless so ugly so fat, she, who has already forgotten how to see herself except through other people's eyes.

At a friend's birthday party, they play hide-and-seek. Her boyfriend pulls her behind one of the heavy living room curtains. They stare at each other. She blushes. He comes closer to her little lips. She closes her eyes, breathless—and then, suddenly, she freezes. Something has coursed through her whole body, gripping her, something disgusting. A coldness, too terrifying to be described.

Disappointed, he will go off and kiss someone else.

Her mother takes her to see her aunt, a nutritionist; she has gained a lot of weight. She's supposed to write down everything she eats in a little notebook, but sometimes she leaves things out, or changes the amounts. She finishes the food on everyone else's plate when no one can see her, eating the leftovers instead of throwing them away. She's always the first one up to clear the table, smiling and helpful, off to degrade herself in the kitchen.

Day after day, the jellyfish tentacles spread.

Her mother takes her to a big police station on the banks of the Seine. The policemen show her a binder stuffed with photos of men; she has to look at them carefully, one by one. She wishes she could tell them, *That's him*, but the anonymous faces hold no meaning or memory for her. She's too afraid to ask if all these men, all these hundreds of paper men staring out at her, are pedophiles, too.

In her sixth-grade history class, the students have to do a presentation on a time period of their choosing. She picks the Holocaust. She spends hours at the local library, looking at pictures of meek, dull-eyed skeletons smiling toothlessly at Red Army photographers. She doesn't tell her parents that she's also checked out *Night and Fog*; she waits until she's home alone one afternoon to watch it. Her report is so meticulously detailed that it takes up four hours of class time, and the history teacher calls her parents to express his concern.

She's lively and cheerful when other people are around, and whenever she can escape the prying eyes, she eats. She laughs a lot, maybe even more than before. Her heart is so heavy that when happiness does approach, she jumps in with both feet.

She and her mother go back to the big police station by the Seine again. A police officer takes her into a dark room; on the other side of a windowed partition, five men with wary expressions are lined up facing her, gazing at her. She's very afraid. *It's a one-way mirror*, the policeman reassures her, *they can't see you*. She doesn't understand. *A one-eyed mirror*. She forces herself to smile, to go a little nearer to the window, to look closely at the men. She wants to be helpful, but the faces still don't mean anything to her.

That same day, or maybe it's another day, she has to describe the man in the stairwell. *How was his face shaped? Oval? Long? And what about his hair?* A bizarre catalogue of body parts scrolls by on the screen of a big grey computer: chins, noses, eyes, foreheads, cheeks, mouths, ears, eyebrows. After a lot of hard work on everyone's part they finally come up with a face; a strange face, like a cadaver's face, with no body and no significance attached to it. A face she still doesn't recognize, even after all that.

She receives a Catholic education, which stamps on her memory an image of the Devil and his temptations. Of sin, and the all-seeing eye of God, fixed on her. Of Hell. Lectures on the primacy of the soul teach hatred of the body, rejection of one's feelings. This comforts her; she despises her body, seeing it only as a vehicle imposed on her, a cesspit. She wants desperately to have a pure and virgin soul, united with God, torn away from this body inhabited by Satan.

She masturbates often, in the Latin sense, *manus stupratio*, defiling herself with her hand. She doesn't know when she started doing it, or where she learned these movements, which are always the same. She doesn't know what they're called. She only has to be alone for a moment for the Devil to come and pull down her underpants. Then, she thumps her vulva mechanically, compulsively, with her hand, until it's swollen and painful and she falls into a dazed, boneless torpor. She doesn't tell anyone about it; she knows it's wrong, but she can't keep herself from doing it. She needs the weightless feeling that always comes afterward. In churches she avoids the hollow eyes of the sculpted imps on the capitals of the columns; always watching her, sneering at her. She is one of them. She punishes her body, stuffing it, striking it. She tries to exist outside of it, and she prays, *de profundis clamo ad te Domine*; she prays with all the ardor in her young heart for God to come and help her. *De*

profundis clamo ad te Domine. De profundis clamo ad te Domine.
De profundis clamo, clamo, clamo ad te Domine. De profundis.

She reads *Les Misérables*, and it isn't Cosette's childhood or
Gavroche's death that moves her the most; no, she sobs with
gratitude all through the chapter in which Hugo explains how
the sewers of Paris fertilize the fields of the countryside.

During long road trips she sits in the very back of the family
car, her forehead pressed to the window, her gaze riveted to a
point far in the distance, deep inside herself, in a place where her
thoughts fragment and drift apart, where her daydreams have no
sense or structure. While her parents listen to Radio Classique in
the front and her brother and sisters squabble in the middle row,
sitting in the very back, she is no longer there.

On weekends, she cocoons herself in the silence of her bedroom in their country cottage and reads. Reads everything,
anything, for hours and hours. Sometimes she wrenches herself
away from a book she is in the midst of, and then there is
pain—pain in her throat, in her jaws; so much pain that she
buries her head beneath the pillows and tries to scream it out,
to vomit it out, spit it out, to get it *out* of her body at last; she
opens her mouth as wide as she can until she is exhausted, but
nothing comes out, ever; not even a murmur, no noise at all.
Nothing. So she swallows the pain back down and, nauseated,
goes back to her book. Page by page she consoles herself, and
forgets herself, and flies away.

She tries to be good. To avoid disappointing anyone. She
gets sadder and sadder, and she doesn't know why. She smiles,
and lies, and fools everyone. She feels shame. Above all, she
mustn't ever let anyone realize it; no one must ever guess.
Nothing must ever, ever show.

When she is thirteen years old, a boy French kisses her at a party. Over the moon at being chosen, she applies herself until her tongue aches and her lips are chapped, but soon enough she gets bored. She writes him passionate notes that go unanswered, blind to the discrepancy between her enthusiastic words and the tension in her jaw.

She is very close to her sister, who is three years older. On some nights she helps her sneak out of the house, distracting their parents at the crucial moment while her sister slips from the piano to the front door. She wakes up when her sister comes home, cuddling up in her bed to hear about the evening; the tricks used to get into a nightclub despite being underage; the other girls' outfits, the boys; the hookups and breakups, the excuses of the heart.

She takes drama classes, and gradually develops a passion for the theater, telling anyone who will listen that she's going to be an actress when she grows up. Onstage, she can have a thousand faces; she doesn't have to pretend a thing. She throws herself wholeheartedly into the role of another person; she embodies herself. Onstage, she experiences an intensity and a clarity that she cannot find anywhere else, but which is nothing more, perhaps, than the warmth of being alive.

She doesn't collect words anymore; now, in her ancient

Greek class, she learns to analyze them, to follow their roots, which are tangled up with the history of mankind.

One day, stunned, she suddenly understands the meaning of *pedophile*. Someone who is friends with a child. A phrase that bursts violently back into her memory, a phrase like a punch in the gut, a phrase the wrong way around. A phrase uttered by the man in the stairwell.

I am your friend.

She wants to smash apart her desk, burn the dictionaries, scream out how words lie—but this time, as so many others, as quickly as the fire roars up inside her, she tamps it back down. She is too frightened by these instances of sudden rage to spend time trying to understand them; she stifles them as soon as they appear and then hurries to the kitchen or the nearest bakery, to smother them between two slices of bread.

Though she knows, now, that some things mean the opposite of what they claim to mean, she doesn't yet wonder why someone would choose to use precisely those words.

During the Easter holidays, her family takes a vacation to the recently reunified Eastern half of Germany. They spend a day at the Ravensbrück concentration camp, and as she reads the survivors' accounts, the comforting illusion that malice and brutality are specifically masculine crumbles and falls away. Reading only about the wars waged by men in her school history books, she has naively shielded herself from violence by considering it an exclusively masculine domain. At Ravensbrück, the tales of the cruelty and perversity of the female guards make her blood run cold. Maybe it isn't Satan whispering those filthy ideas in her ear, after all—maybe *she* is really Satan, herself.

Sometimes, sitting silently on her bed, legs stretched out in front of her like foreign objects, she studies this body of hers perplexedly, pinching it as if the pain will prove that it really belongs to her. She doesn't recognize it.

And often, when her mind is on something else, she sees him. He's on the floor a few meters away from her, a pile of detached body parts. These images don't frighten her; she doesn't question them or wonder about them. She simply copes.

During PE, her body weighs her down. She hates the taste of blood in the back of her throat when she runs; she hates her flushed cheeks; she hates it when her mind is too overwhelmed with physical sensation to think of anything else. She almost never manages to catch a pass; when she sees the ball coming toward her, she freezes. In dance class, her mind is so often elsewhere that she can never memorize the choreography, so she slips to the back of the class where no one will see her copying others' movements.

When they go out to the athletic field—I should mention that this is a private Catholic school where girls make up the vast majority of the student body, and the few male students are treated like demigods—on the edge of the Bois de Boulougne, it's usually the same two or three exhibitionists who come and expose their cocks to the rows of young girls.

On those days, she prays that there won't be an endurance race; that the teacher won't start the class with an embarrassed muttering of *Okay, okay, okay, finish the race, all the way now, just don't look.* Because then, with every stride that brings her closer to them, imagining their eyes on her, imagining them because she can't see them, because her gaze is firmly fixed on the ochre-colored ground of the track, she feels dirty; so dirty, her flushed skin sizzling, signaling it to everyone, to them, the ones licking their lips. Here comes the first curve; she hasn't raised her head, it's a major achievement that she's even still breathing. She passes in front of them; she can feel, all over her body, their menacing eyes their hard hands their sweaty penises, but they haven't moved, they're still on the other side of the fence. She keeps running; she feels like she's moving in slow motion, like she has to wrench the soles of her shoes off the ground. Another curve; she hates her thighs for trembling so much, for giving those men something to watch, and the further away she gets, the more easily she can breathe. Another curve, and another, and it all starts over, going past them again and again. Soon she can't feel anything at all anymore, and she wonders how her legs can keep running without her.

In tenth grade she dates an older boy, an eleventh-grader. They're alone at his house, and he takes her to his parents' room, where they stretch out awkwardly on the bed together, kissing, pressing their bodies together, breathing. They're afraid and hot and full of desire. He pulls down her panties and touches her vulva with his fingers. He has hardly slid the underpants along her legs when she freezes; something breaks and spreads inside her, something filthy, filling her vagina and her throat; he has hardly touched her vulva when she suddenly feels so much pure hate that she could beat him to death. An instant later, she isn't there anymore. He stops, sheepish and shamefaced before her motionless body. She excuses herself, gets dressed, and leaves. She breaks up with him the next day, over the phone.

There is a new girl in her class, Sigrid, who has purple Doc Martens and a devastating sense of humor. The two of them, along with Marine, who is repeating the school year, and whose father killed her mother with a rifle when she was little, and whose insolence and wit all the other students admire, form a tight-knit trio. They each belong to different groups of friends, but they often slip away to spend a few hours together at a café, solving the world's problems, smoking, honing their rebellious minds, and laughing, laughing at everything, these three girls who understand each other so perfectly, who loved each other right away.

Marine never talks about her childhood, much of which was spent in prison visiting rooms, or about the return home a few months ago of the father/murderer. Marine is a blazing inferno of joy and intelligence.

Adélaïde never talks about the man in the stairwell. She never thinks about it. She lives just a few meters above where it happened, on the next floor up; every day she is more cheerful, more fearless. She twists and twirls and laughs, and never stays in one place.

Sigrid confides that her older sister was raped and killed by the Beast of the Bastille five years ago. She isn't looking for condolences and doesn't expect them to say anything; she mentions it only once, in the interest of honesty.

Bubbly, sparkling Marine dies two days after the school year ends, of a combination of anorexia, alcohol, sleeping pills, and irreparable sadness.

Sigrid transfers to a different school, and they lose touch.

Years later, the French National DNA Database, which Sigrid's father helps to launch, will turn my life upside down.

I will think back on our unlikely trio, our Amazonian desires, our madcap dreams; our pure, wolfish joy.

A t the very end of summer vacation, she is driving a moped, her best friend clinging to her waist from behind, when a flower-delivery truck comes barreling around a bend in the road. She lies motionless with skull and wrist fractures and head trauma, five front teeth knocked out. Her friend, horrified, is unharmed.

She is put in intensive care. In this room broken up by sliding curtains you can hear your neighbors but not see them, and the hours roll by to the comforting rhythm of many hearts hospitalized together. One day, a few meters away from her, one of those hearts speeds up horribly. Footsteps pound, and the heart stops, and the bed is taken away. And one night, she is the one that goes.

No words can capture that between-two-worlds sojourn they call a *near-death experience*, for lack of a better term. I've tried to explain it occasionally, but how can you describe the timelessness, the infinity, the intangibility, the sweetness? How can you tell it in a few sentences; sum it up without diminishing it somehow, without putting it in too small a box, without making it seem too tame? But yes, it was the most purely joyous moment of my entire existence, and knowing I'll get to go back again someday is a source of deep consolation on my bad days.

What brought me back to life that night was feeling, with a

vividness that exceeded the senses—feeling in my mouth, my throat, the explosive sweetness of biting into a crisp apple. Feeling, in my nostrils and all through my windpipe, the scent of pine needles rolled between my fingertips. Feeling the vibrant moistness of a handful of damp soil against my palm.

Then, I sank into a heavy sleep.

When she wakes up, her body has inexplicably regained its full range of motion. When she wakes up, she's afraid. Thinking you're God is a sure sign that you've gone crazy. She withdraws into herself. What she saw that night can't have been real, so . . . what? So, she's crazy. So, she keeps the loving light and the softness and the immensity to herself. When she wakes up, she doesn't mention them to anyone.

Her condition stabilizes, and she is moved from intensive care to a room on the neurology ward. She'd really like to get a look at her face, but her mother claims she's forgotten her compact and the nurses insist that the mirrors in the corridor are all screwed into the walls and can't be moved.

One night, she manages to slip out of bed. Holding her IV bags in her shaky arms, she switches on the bathroom light. Someone looks back at her from the mirror, someone with a blue and swollen face and a bleeding hole of a mouth.

After that her smile is courtesy of a dental plate—which forces her, at the age of fifteen and a half, to stop sucking her thumb. Her mother had tried everything to make her stop the babyish habit; bitter-tasting nail polish, bandaging her thumbs, and even a guinea pig—a gift conditional on her stopping completely, but the guinea pig had quickly ended up being eaten by a neighborhood cat and she had resumed the habit, ashamed and soothed by this comfort that was within arm's reach and yet forbidden.

Back in school, she swaps her tight jeans and high heels for soft sweaters, loose-fitting trousers, and oversized plaid button-down shirts that she is constantly tugging over her bottom. She wears her strawberry-blond hair pulled back in a tight bun.

Every time she passes a window or a mirror, she hates herself. When her mother and sisters take her shopping, she bursts into tears in the dressing room. She would love to look like them, but every pair of trousers she tries on is too tight, or won't button, or if it does button, the waist gapes so much that a belt can't fix it. She never buys anything.

She can't concentrate in class; she focuses on the teachers' expressions, her notes on grid-lined paper, her pen; she sketches contorted faces in the margins and fills in the silences, the empty spaces. She grips her desk, she resists, but every time the soundless black wave washes over her without warning and she slips down to float, suspended, in some distant netherworld.

One evening, friends of her parents react to some story or other by laughing and saying *Oh, Adélaïde, the alien of the family!* No one suspects how that phrase wounds her, she who is living separated from all of them; she, who wants nothing more than to be one of them.

She spends the school year crying in the girls' bathroom, bingeing and purging, hating herself ferociously and, in public, flashing her dental-plate smile, getting good grades, playing the part of the courageous girl. This is the year she starts hitting herself, thumping her head with her fists, banging it against walls, devising scenarios for perfect suicides, suicides disguised as accidents, suicides no one would suspect. She doesn't speak to anyone about her ideas, her jellyfish; she tries to confine them strictly to a crude and opaque world.

She convinces herself that she is made up of two completely separate parts: the disgusting, treacherous body, and the pure, bright, joyous mind.

At the end of eleventh grade, the high school gives them a choice between a silent retreat at the convent of Bec-Hellouin and a tour of the Loire Valley castles. Three days and two nights. She is obscurely aware that she won't be able to keep up her act for that long in front of her friends, so she is the only one to choose the silence of the convent.

On one endless, hopeless night, chanting *De profundis clamo ad te Domine* alone in a tiny chapel, someone sits down next to her and gently puts an arm around her shoulders—the white yeti, Jesus, whoever. Someone. Her sadness drains away, like the water in a reservoir when the floodgates are opened.

Until the next downpour.

At a friend's country house, she often finds herself alone with a couple of other girls. One night, the oldest one teaches the rest how to masturbate. She explains where to find the clitoris; that you have to be very gentle, rubbing in little circles, wetting your fingers with saliva if you have to; to slow down, to speed up, to play with it. *Here, I'll show you.* She pulls a blanket over herself, and they can see the subtle to-and-fro movement of her hand under its folds. Her fingers emerge briefly so she can wet them in her mouth; she grows pink-cheeked and breathless. Eyes half-closed, her movements accelerate, and she moans and shudders, features contorting, head thrown back. Then, silence. Her face is slack, relaxed. She opens large, shining eyes and looks at the astonished faces of the other girls, smiling, hair mussed, proud of the effect she has clearly made.

Stupefaction. Other girls do this, and it isn't evil, or shameful? It's normal? The relief is overwhelming.

She tries to duplicate the other girl's artlessness and confidence later, when she's alone, but she can't do it. Gentle caresses don't do anything for her; they aren't hard enough. She prefers to be struck. *What she does is useless; it doesn't work for me.* What works for her has nothing to do with pleasure. What works is being violent enough with herself that she leaves her weak, spineless body and goes somewhere else, where she doesn't feel anything, where she can float, where she no longer exists. And then loathing herself. Being disgusted by herself. Hating herself.

She doesn't understand that there are two irreconcilable states of being, two opposing extremes often lumped together into the same word: *masturbation*. For her friends it's about feeling alive in their bodies, about pleasure and excitement. For her, it's about the absent body, inflammation, and contempt.

In my family we never talk about our bodies, except maybe to make fun of them. My dad almost died of blood poisoning recently, a condition he treated, cheerfully, with his usual remedy: four heavy blankets, an aspirin, and a few days in bed. In my family, talking about little aches and pains is just undignified. And talking about sex? Talking about that? About what she did when she was sure nobody would come in, nobody could see her, in the silence of her bedroom, hidden in the woods, perched in a tree, locked in a bathroom? In the terrifying and increasingly degrading scenarios she used to come up with then?

She's convinced her high school drama teacher to put on Giraudoux's *Ondine*, with her in the title role. As soon as she can, she takes herself out to the Île aux Cygnes in the Seine, under the Bir Hakeim Bridge. Here, she *is* Ondine, the water nymph—a monster, maybe, but a beguiling, fairylike one, and this is her kingdom, this slip of land in the great river. She murmurs long soliloquies to the weeping willows; she populates the shallows with handsome mermen; she has long hair that covers her breasts; and the insanity of this desperate attempt to disappear into someone else becomes cruelly apparent on the night of the premiere, when she freezes up in the middle of a line in Act I. Someone offstage whispers the words to her but she doesn't respond. A pause, and then the stage lights are turned off. When enough time has passed for her to slip off into the wings, the lights come up again, and she hasn't moved.

They begin Act II, embarrassed—and suddenly she is on the floor, convulsing. She wakes up in the hospital, dazed. Her beautiful siren's costume glitters pointlessly against the hard mattress. They explain to her that she's had an epileptic fit, a common complication after the kind of severe head trauma she suffered last year. She doesn't say it, but she knows exactly what caused the *grand mal*: she disobeyed. She wanted too much from life, and this was her punishment.

At seventeen she dates an older guy. He wants to make love, which reassures her that he knows how to do it, that he's done it before.

He's put clean sheets on the bed and lit a candle. She takes her clothes off and sits on the edge of the bed. Completely naked, she shivers with cold. He lies down with her, kisses her, asking *Are you okay? I'm not hurting you, am I?* She jumps, startled; she was miles away, again. *Uh, no, no, I'm fine, you aren't hurting me.* In truth, she doesn't feel anything, anything at all; she's bored, and doesn't know what to do with her hands.

They do it regularly after that and, every time, she leaves her body and goes somewhere else. She tells herself that sex is really something you do for men anyway; it must be normal for the girl not to feel anything. He is bewildered by the unresponsiveness of her body; he asks questions, trying to find out what she likes. She doesn't know what to tell him. She doesn't want to disappoint him. It's great, she says; she loves it, and even *It was cool when we did it on the floor.*

She asks a girlfriend for advice; the little noises she should make, the facial expressions, the movements, and applies the lessons conscientiously, mimicking the pleasure, the moans. She fills the time. She avoids looking at him or touching his penis. The idea disgusts her. None of that interests her. Flesh, physical sensation—they're crude, primitive. Literature and philosophy are what she loves, and she reads everything she can get her hands on. She gets high honors on her university entrance exam, and in two months she'll begin a two-year undergraduate degree program.

They break up when the summer ends, but they still see each other from time to time. *Do you still not like it?* he asks a year or two later. No, she informs him dryly, she's above all of that; *he* is really obsessed. He looks at her with a gentle, sad expression she doesn't understand, and which she will think about sometimes, years later.

When the first year of her degree program begins, she measures her vanity and ignorance against towering library shelves filled entirely with books belonging to the program and her notes in beginner's Latin, minus forty-five out of twenty. She meets four great girls who will join in her heart the five loyal friends she has had since high school.

Her mother takes her to a new nutritionist. She's too chubby, and steamed vegetables, grated carrots with lemon juice, and fat-free yogurts don't seem to be making a difference. Once again, she is silent about her binges; she refuses to take them into account, to give them too much life by talking about them. She lies to the people around her, just as she lies to herself.

This year, she stops forcing herself to vomit. When she sticks her fingers deeply down her throat, the bad feelings the act awakens in her are worse than the ones she's trying to soothe.

She starts writing things down in a notebook with a sky-blue cover; it's a way to get her morbid thoughts out on paper, a record of her own self-loathing. She writes to tame the jelly-fish, to keep them from stinging.

She spends her Easter vacation having a sliver of bone from her skull grafted onto her upper jaw, which has become shockingly necrotic since the accident.

Her face swells until her eyes and nostrils are all but invisible; she looks like a hippopotamus some Fauvist painter has brightened up by painting it purple and yellow. She likes to gaze at the hippopotamus in the mirror. There is something extremely reassuring and honest about her deformity; with this face, she can finally be herself. But the graft doesn't take, and her classic bourgeois features soon rose to the surface again.

It's a study-focused year until the bone graft, after which she is absolutely determined to become an actress. She hasn't set foot onstage since *Ondine*, and now those feet are itching. The fire that illuminates her from within when she's acting threatens to devour her when she isn't, and without the boards to contain it, it consumes her.

She leaves to spend the whole summer working as a counsellor at a girls' camp in Canada. For several years she is lucky enough to spend an entire month deep in Algonquin Provincial Park, exploring its many lakes and roasting marshmallows over a campfire, and in the crackling of the pine needles and the hooting of the loons, in the bursts of laughter and songs, in all the nights spent contemplating the Milky Way with her friends, she experiences sisterhood and trust. There, the jellyfish are still and quiet; she is truly happy, caring, and capable. There, no one needs a mask, and everyone works to be the best version of themselves. There, the bonds of friendship she forms are unbreakable. There, she is *Addy*, her vibrant and luminous twin. A good girl. She devours these days with the appetite for life of a prisoner on furlough, and every year when the summer ends, she sobs and grits her teeth on the flight home.

This time, she gains twenty pounds in two months. Her parents don't recognize her at the airport; their gazes skim over this fat American in a hooded sweatshirt. She has to wave her arms and call out to them before they finally spot her in the crowd.

That fall she enrolls at the Sorbonne rather than moving on to the second half of her two-year degree. Twice a week, in a conservatory, she prepares to sit the competitive entrance exam to study dramatic arts at one of several prestigious universities. She eats, breathes, and sleeps one word: *theater*. The other drama students already seem to know all about this world that is so strange and new to her; the great directors, the contemporary playwrights they've all read but her, the shows that shouldn't have been missed—so she makes up for lost time, seeing a play almost every night. She forms devoted friendships with some other passionate young people, all from less privileged backgrounds and all of whom have come up to Paris in pursuit of the same dream: going on the Stage.

She's relieved to have found her path because, secretly, she has thought more than once that she might be called to take up Holy Orders. And maybe the convent and the stage, the saint and the excommunicate all strike the same chord in her, the same desire to sacrifice herself, to deny herself, to find meaning outside of herself.

Today, when I hear about priests who sexually abuse children on the radio, I think of that terrified young girl, that girl who hated herself so much that God's unconditional love for her overwhelmed her with gratitude. I think about her tears in churches, about her desperate prayers, about the words she repeated over and over and over, *De profundis clamo ad te Domine*. She wanted, sometimes, to dedicate her life to Him, gradually to achieve clarity and calmness of mind, to confine her unclean body within a cell, and along with it the jellyfish that came and went within her, and which she can only think of as *demons*.

Priesthood, abstinence, religion—those aren't what create serial child molesters, no. I really don't think so. But of the countless numbers of abused children, how many grow up to become priests, or take vows of abstinence, or embrace religion, as a safeguard against insanity? God isn't trained to manage the psycho-traumatic consequences of sexual violence. God can't keep away the filthy, surging thoughts. I know. I prayed for it often enough. I think it's just that some of the ones who have sought refuge in the cloth in an attempt to feel less worthless stop loathing themselves, and start hating and controlling others instead—and then, yes, they take advantage of their profession, with its built-in aura of saintliness, and the carefully controlled silence of its structures, to violate and destroy in their turn, with full impunity.

She goes out with a young pharmacist for a couple of months. He is very loving, very gentle, going down on her for hours every night, trying to make her moan. She doesn't understand why he's wearing himself out for nothing. Sex is a waste of time. Sex is boring. She is nineteen years old.

He is the first person she tells about what happened to her that night after the accident, the between-two-worlds episode she can't explain. A few days later, browsing idly in the social sciences section at Fnac, she stumbles across a book on *near-death experiences*. What? This happened to other people; there are other stories about it? God! She isn't completely crazy after all.

She sets about reading all kinds of books about life after death, reincarnation, past lives, angels, prophecies, shamanism, and altered states of consciousness.

She learns to roll joints and drink alcohol. She loves the cheeky, funny girl who takes her place when she drinks.

One evening, she goes to a play about the love of a mature woman for a very young boy and the qualms suffered by the female judge who sentenced her. The theater is small and dusty, with the audience seated on benches just a few feet from the actress, and the longer the performance goes on, the harder she finds it to breathe. She wants to stop the whole thing, to scream and sing at the top of her lungs, to knock over the benches, but she can't even manage to stand up and leave.

On the way home, she scribbles in her notebook, with its cover as blue as the sky, the story of a May day when she was nine years old, of what she calls the bad memory, the event, the ( ). *All of a sudden I'm transported into the body of that little girl,* she writes, *even though it's so different from the body I have now. Everything is so precise, like a series of photographs. I remember it all exactly as it happened, but in a slightly odd, detached way.*

She doesn't know that there are some photos missing from her story, and that it will take her years to rediscover them intact.

Shortly after that night, she finds that she can't act anymore. She, who used to find it so easy to slip into someone else's skin, suddenly finds that she is ACTING, and she's appalled. She overdoes it; she lays it on too thick; she speaks too loud or too softly. She monitors herself. She isolates herself.

The jellyfish are multiplying now, twining themselves freely through the cracks between her thoughts, and beneath their large red umbrellas are thousands of stinging tentacles loaded with tiny, poisonous phrases: *I am worthless, I am fat, I can't do anything, I'm a bad person.*

Sometimes, without warning, when she's doing something else, when she doesn't notice the school gathering around her, closing in on her, she suddenly feels as if she's being sucked into the depths.

Her binges get more extreme and more frequent, sometimes two or even three a day. In her sky-blue notebook she calls herself *the goatskin of fat, the lard balloon, the pig.* She thinks her body is filled with pus. She imagines herself cutting into the fat, sees it spilling over the scissors, the blades thrusting into it, fat spurting out. She thinks about it, but she doesn't do it. If she has scars or Band-Aids, people will find out.

Her drama teacher feels that she hasn't found her voice, so she looks for a vocal instructor. Someone recommends an opera singer well-versed in esotericism who teaches skeletal resonance and vocal yoga.

Soon she can't bear to miss these lessons, during which nothing comes out of her but hoarse yowling, stifled screams, and sobs, and from which she always emerges relieved and serene. She is convinced that she's on a spiritual journey, and that all her sufferings are initiation rites, stages leading to full consciousness. If her pain is merely the scum left over from previous lives then she can't be crazy, she reassures herself.

She smokes pot more and more often. In the evenings she makes up a batch of mini-spliffs which she then stores in a metal box, smoking the first one in the early hours of the morning, as soon as she arrives at the university, before her first class. It helps her to forget herself, to let herself float, and it means that her friends are less surprised by her moments of blankness.

She surrounds herself with soothing objects and rituals. She buys herself shoes that look friendly, round-toed and smiling, and explains them with comforting stories, such as her *hyperspace sewage-worker boots*: mid-calf-length boots in green leather which she wears almost every day despite her girlfriends' skepticism. Year after year she buys the same daily planner with bible paper and black leather covers; she uses the same small, soft-bound, grid-lined notebooks: dark-blue for class notes, sky blue for her private journals, and red for creative writing. In the red notebooks, she writes almost nothing.

In conversations she embellishes her life, adding a bit of drama and suspense, making up cozy little arrangements with reality to suit herself, backing up her stories with anecdotes as juicy as they are false. The tales are often novel-like in both detail and unbelievability, and her friends make excuses for her, smiling at what they call *Adélaïde's enchanted world*. Having people listen to her makes her feel like she exists, so she invents herself as fast as everything passes her by.

Her room is in the attic, directly below the roof, and she figures out that, by pushing a chair against the radiator and using it as a step-stool to climb out the window, she can access a gently sloping ledge that ends in a low stone wall, which looks sort of like a large moustache covered with zinc. She suns herself there, smokes cigarettes and joints, and writes. On the barren days, the days when jellyfish contaminate the horizon, she seats herself on top of the moustache, her movements as rigid and precise as those of some antique robot. The surface is about twenty centimeters square; her buttocks bulge over the sides, and her feet dangle above the void. Perched on the seventh floor, fearsome and calm, she balances quietly. All she would have to do is let herself slip to either side, or lean forward, and everything would be over.

She is twenty, and often, when crossing a street, she is hypnotized by the ballet of the cars, by this human body of hers waltzing from car body to car body, and then coming apart under the black tires. These visions of herself in pieces have been her companions for too long to frighten her anymore; no, what terrifies her is that she will let her guard down and a jellyfish will drag her down for real, forever, beneath the wheels, over the rails, out the windows. So, she curses herself, she slaps herself, she bites her own wrists, and waits against a wall until someone arrives whose steps she can match with her own until she reaches the other side of the street safe and sound. In the metro, she presses herself against the platform walls. She no longer dares to go near the windows on the upper floors of a building.

When she's with her friends she is happy, smiling, full of enthusiasm and hearty laughter. *If they knew, they'd run away with their tails between their legs*. She has trouble accepting compliments. She is always alert, always wary, wondering what a man is expecting, what he wants from her. If he seems sincere, she is filled with scorn. *Is he blind, or what?*

She passes the entrance exam for the École supérieure d'art dramatique de la Ville de Paris, ESAD, thanks to a scene in which her only job was to reflect a girlfriend's pure joy in acting. She gives up her master's courses at the university and stops work on her thesis on *The Idea of the Monster in the Myth of Ondine.*

The day after the attack on the World Trade Center in New York, she seeks refuge in the Church of Saint-Eustache. She has seen too many terrible images, too many horrors; she wants, for just a few moments, to suspend in the blue sky those people she sees falling whenever she closes her eyes. She lights an altar candle and kneels; she weeps and prays fervently for a long time, but something keeps disturbing her, forcing her back to the surface, something—no, *someone*, someone watching her. A man, thirtyish, is standing in the middle of the nave, zipper down, penis exposed. He stares at her, and smiles, and jerks off.

The next day she bravely goes back to the church, wanting to warn the sacristan. He hasn't seen anything but doesn't seem very surprised. *If you only knew how many weirdos come into churches*, he sighs.

Soon afterward, during a singing exercise, while she is throwing back her shoulders and pushing out her chest, she suddenly begins howling, a long, harsh sound that goes on and on and breaks into sobs. She doesn't scream she vomits out the rage she spits out the pain she ends up panting and dazed on her hands and knees on the Persian carpet. The teacher is dumbfounded, and at their next session firmly suggests that she seek help, handing her the number of a psychotherapist.

She doesn't call. She can't bring herself to do it.

She is passionate about what she's learning at ESAD; she makes new friends and a handsome young man from the year above her kisses her one evening, murmuring that he's wanted to do it for a long time. She is swept off her feet by his tenderness and sensitivity. He is in love with her, and his hands tame her and soothe her little by little. He reads Fromm's *The Art of Love* to her, picturing her in a long white cotton dress, running through a field of ripe wheat. She isn't always sure she's really the person he's imagining, but it doesn't matter; he's so handsome, and so sweet.

One night, when she's smoked enough grass to part her thighs for the caress of his tongue, she allows herself to be carried away for the first time on soft and powerful waves. Her body bucks reflexively, breathless and pink-cheeked, her mind spinning, quivering, moaning, incandescent, her hands busy and full of life, and she suddenly wants him desperately. The words *desire,* and *orgasm* aren't empty ones for her after that, but they will remain rare.

The better her life gets, the deeper she is in over her head. The schools of jellyfish surge up without leaving her time to arm herself against them; she breaks down in class, in the street, in her lover's arms. Happy days are bracketed by dark ones. She stops trying to convince herself that it's just a side effect of her emotional chakras opening, that it will pass, that she's getting better. Her personality changes constantly; she's afraid she might be bipolar, schizophrenic, manic depressive, delusional. She's afraid she won't dare to tell a psychotherapist anything. She's afraid she'll be institutionalized if she tells one everything. And she's afraid there might be nothing wrong with her at all; afraid of lying to herself, holding her own head underwater to escape her own crass mediocrity, her conformism.

She wishes she could talk to her parents about it, but she can't. She plays the role of the perfect daughter with a brilliant smile to perfection, while they attribute her lined face on the dark mornings to the turbulent moodiness of an emerging *artiste*. She suffers from the forced isolation and the lack of honesty in her family, but she doesn't know how to cross this ocean of suppressed tears. She's exhausted from placing one foot in front of the other, from putting on a body every morning that sags across the bed like a coat on a hanger, from dragging herself through each day and falling asleep at night with the anguished awareness that time is passing, quickly, and it isn't waiting for her.

S he calls the psychotherapist the day after her twenty-first birthday. He doesn't have room for any new patients in his schedule at the moment, but she apologizes so fervently that he agrees to see her for one session anyway.

Getting to his office involves a key code, a heavy metal door, a long, cobbled passage, and then, suddenly, a tranquil and luxurious inner courtyard patrolled by a big grey Chartreux cat that weaves between her calves, meowing. The office itself is a single-story bungalow entered with no prior notice, no bowing and scraping. It's a small room whose walls are covered with egg-cartons, the meticulous additions of a cellist in search of perfect acoustics. A pull-out sofa bed, a few cushions, a box of tissues, a wicker garbage basket—and, facing them, a chair, in which a kind-faced man sits, looking at her.

She has barely sat down when she bursts into tears, and cries for a solid hour without managing to put a full sentence together. The next day she sends him a postcard with a picture of an Egyptian statue whose face has been destroyed by blows of a chisel. On the back she has written simply, *Thank you.*

He refers her to a young therapist with a heavily rounded belly, who glows with that radiant self-assurance pregnant women sometimes have. Their sessions take place in a long room overlooking the street, a rectangle of beige carpet with cheap mattresses and faded cushions against the walls, feebly lit by a row of cathedral-glass windows. The door opens directly onto a perpetually dirty sidewalk.

This woman specializes in *transgenerational trauma*, the subconscious inheritance of unresolved grief and trauma experienced by previous generations; so, for the next session she has to draw up a family tree, to which she will add the family events she thinks are the most significant.

She completes the task carefully and doesn't see anything terribly interesting about it, until the psychotherapist underlines thirteen times in thick red ink the words: *fall, overturned, defenestration.* She has retained nothing about people's lives except accidents, illnesses, suicides. In her own brief life so far, nine falls. And *sexual touching*.

She brushes off this episode quickly: *I was lucky; it was only touching, and my parents reacted in just the right way. They realized that something was wrong and questioned me about it, and then called the police. I don't think that's the cause of my problems; I never think about it. How does it make me feel now, to think about it? Um . . . no particular feelings. I don't really feel one way or another about it. Besides, even on the day it happened, I'd already stopped crying by the time they put me in the police car; I remember smiling when they turned on the revolving lights.* The psychotherapist: *You developed a pattern of resistance to pain very early. You're going to have to work on that eventually.*

Around her friends she radiates cheerfulness, and if she reveals anything it is only a few superficial words now and then. She never lingers; she runs, she is scattered, she goes in a thousand different directions every day. The darker and more despairing she feels in the depths of her soul, the more aglow she is to the outside world, a will-o'-the-wisp.

She's had an odd cough for the past few months, a frog in her throat that her daily vocal exercises can't chase away. With her family and her boyfriend her voice is as high-pitched as a little girl's, irritating and false, while onstage it deepens, taking on weight and softness. It annoys her; she's well aware that neither of these voices is really hers. She doesn't know where the real one is.

One evening after smoking a joint, she sketches in her dark-blue notebook the two positions her body usually adopts. She's almost always in one or the other of them, she has noticed; standing, sitting, at home, at school, on the bus or the metro. Then, in a long paragraph, she analyses how these positions are clearly suggestive of *intuitive energetic readjustment.*

Both of the rigid silhouettes are headless and footless. One of them has its arms crossed tightly over its chest, left fist clenched, covering its genitals, the right hand clasping the left. The other figure grips its lower abdomen with one arm and crushes its breasts with the other. A constrained body, an ashamed body, a hated body.

At the end of her first year at the École supérieure d'art dramatique, one professor says her acting is false and superficial; another tells her she needs to get deeper into her sexuality. In her notebook she wonders dispiritedly, *How do you get deeper into your sexuality???*

She kicks off the summer with a second bone graft from her skull to her jaw; the procedure successfully takes this time, but she wakes up completely exhausted. She doesn't much like anything that summer, especially herself. She binge-eats to forget, to sink into the plump rolls of her own belly fat, to become a gelatinous, useless mass, a huge jellyfish washed up on a rock. She dumps her tender and attentive boyfriend; their hideous love repulses her.

A summer spent loathing herself so deeply, thinking so constantly of suicide, finally pushes her one evening, at the very end of her tether, to talk to her worried parents. She manages to put a little of her loneliness into words, her feelings of inadequacy, her suffering—but she hides the hate, the violence, the psychotherapy. They listen to her; they don't judge her; they console her, and enfold her gently in their arms. It has been so long since they allowed themselves to do that.

By the time classes begin again, her psychotherapist has moved out to the distant suburbs. She writes to her several times, *strongly recommending* the therapy group (three hours every Thursday night) led by the initial therapist she visited in the same long room overlooking a dirty street. Telling her that, *above all, she mustn't stop in the middle of treatment.* That she is *concerned by her silence.*

She isn't especially attracted to the idea of telling her despair-filled stories to despair-filled strangers, and doesn't reply to the psychotherapist's letters, or her phone calls.

She has a string of relationships that last only a few nights, and her girlfriends diagnose her with an advanced case of *Batman/Joker syndrome.* Every time she meets a new guy she's absolutely sure he's the love of her life, the future father of her children, the eighth wonder of the world—and then all it takes is the tiniest thing—the smell of his sweat, an awkward movement, an overly affectionate phrase—for Batman to fall through a trap door and the Joker to rise up and take his place. In a heartbeat she changes from the lovestruck, sensual woman to a cold fish. Fortunately, she doesn't sleep with every Batman she meets; many of them never know what has happened between them behind the curtains of her closed eyelids. Her readiness to fall for anyone who looks at her twice carries a huge amount of risk, like the time a young house painter traps her at his place and she barely manages to escape a violent assault, fleeing under a barrage of insults.

*

At school, her voice teacher tells her that her voice is trapped in the back of her throat, that she isn't letting it resonate, isn't giving anything of herself. He talks about a fog that the sound does not penetrate; so, at each lesson, she tries valiantly to find her vocal cords, but she can't feel them, or tell where they are. It makes her want to bang her head against a wall, as if the whole front of her throat was missing.

Shortly before Christmas there is another round of dental surgery, a new period of feeling empty and beaten down. She resolves to go to the therapy group.

In her sky-blue notebook: *Confused the day after; it seems like my neuroses are too complicated just to be blamed on my parents. And anyway, why is it so important for me to understand and explain everything? It's all much bigger than us.*

The next week: *Great session last night. Three hours of sobbing and convulsing and internal earthquakes. This morning I feel light as a feather!*

And the week after that: *Well, here I am again, lost in the depths of my soul. I don't know anything anymore; it's all endorphins, I've been excruciatingly calm lately. Who's whispering behind me? How can I protect myself? What kind of dragon's den is this? What monsters will I have to battle next, and which princesses will I have to save?*

She is twenty-two years old the next spring, and mired in the same rut of suffering and solitude. When she's alone she hits herself, since she can't cut herself; warm-weather clothes show too much of the body, and her mother would see the marks. When she's around other people she smokes cigarettes to give herself something to do with her hands, smokes weed to turn off her thoughts, drinks alcohol to lighten herself up. She discovers ecstasy, magic mushrooms, and all the incredibly funny and affectionate girls she becomes when she's no longer herself.

She spends her group therapy meetings in tears, unable to transform her sobs into words. When the therapist offers to treat her in individual sessions, she gladly returns to the pretty courtyard with the cat that winds between her feet and the funny office with its egg-carton-covered walls.

There is another operation before summer comes; this time the surgeon opens up her new jaw, which is barely a year old, to screw in implants for five new teeth. She stares at the reflection in the adjustable chrome lamp of her gaping maw and the surgeon's hands busy inside it. She doesn't recognize herself. That dark hole cannot possibly be her mouth.

She spends the summer swimming, becoming one with the wide blue expanse, letting herself be carried along on the waves, listening underwater to the world's crystalline echo, feeling her long hair drift and dance around her.

One evening she writes in her sky-blue notebook, after suffering a deep cut to her foot: *Taken all together, the string of stupid accidents I've had in my short life could swallow me like a boa constrictor. Always the same symptoms repeating themselves, accidents, obsessive thoughts of death, general lassitude, incessant self-criticism, lack of a distinct identity, cyclothymia, doubts, and self-loathing. And I still don't get any of it, except, I know it won't ever stop until I do understand. But shit, what is there to understand? I'm so tired of running on this carpet that keeps endlessly rolling up on itself.*

When autumn arrives again, in her dark-blue notebook she writes a list of *Resolutions for the new academic year:*
Stop jutting my neck forward when I'm acting
Throaty voice
Overacting
Stop looking like a plaster mask of the angel Gabriel (why am I so afraid of living?)

She has yet another operation just before Christmas. This time they're going to make room in her gums for the implants; slice open with a scalpel skin that has barely scarred over from the last time, weave in and out with a needle, pull hard on the thread. She spends the whole night before the procedure trembling; she can't bear this strange mouth anymore, heavy and clumsy after anesthesia, and the fingers inside it cutting, thumping, sewing.

For the whole month afterward, she can't even break the surface to breathe.

She works hard at ESAD. She's making progress; the instructors watch her carefully: *Where are your legs? Get out of the control tower and come down into your body, Adélaïde!*

*

The dance teacher introduces the students to the Feldenkrais Method. Lying on the floor, you have to make tiny movements, welcoming and exploring attentively all physical sensations: how the left arm communicates with the right leg; how the knee has a thousand hitherto-unknown ways to bend; how the feet know how to make the head nod or shake.

She finds it absolutely new, and incredibly difficult. Her body, that old, clumpy pile of dying cells, her body, a wild and mysterious continent? She begins the first round of negotiations in the peace process.

When the stomach cramps hit, and a lump rises in her throat, she breathes, concentrates, plays for time: first isolating herself, anywhere no one can see her—bedrooms, kitchens, bathrooms, churches, porches; any nook will do. Then, curled in on herself, she lets the jellyfish in, screaming without making a sound, hands clamped over her wide-open mouth, swaying, racking her brain for some image filthy enough to make her freeze and go cold, calm. Still shaky, she stands up and splashes water on her face (if it's holy water, well, too bad), massages her jaw, opens her eyes wide, pinches her cheeks, straightens her hair . . . and starts all over again.

In the street, in bars, at parties, she is constantly on her guard, starting and jumping, staring, listening, taking note. The guy over there with the shifty eyes. The other one who won't turn around, and she can't manage to edge behind him. She's suspicious of all of them. Her girlfriends complain that she's only listening to them with half an ear; that she never remembers their stories, and it's true; often she just catches the last few words, only to ask another question whose answer she won't listen to either, so absorbed is she in *watching out*.

Sober, she's incapable of relaxing. Drunk or drugged, she

immediately tries to seduce the guy who made her so uncomfortable before. She prefers to play on the brink of the abyss. She's calmer when she's afraid.

The jellyfish multiply the morning after. One Sunday on the roof, she moves forward, resolved to fall; just one more step, and . . . a tiny, meaningless little thing, a breath of wind, and she shivers, and backs away. After that day she stays away from hard drugs, indulging only on special occasions, and only when she knows she won't spend the next day alone.

She's a regular at a squat occupied by friends, where they rehearse, and play, and have incredible parties. She meets an array of appalling strangers there whom, as soon as she has drunk something, she hits on aggressively—like the guy leaning his elbows on the kitchen counter, ogling her like a butcher assessing a carcass. With that false, terrible casualness she adopts mechanically in cases like this, she accosts him and chats him up, and he looks her up and down, nudges closer to her, gropes her playfully. Unluckily he is one of the regulars; she sees him again at every party after that, and each time, without understanding why she does it, she forces herself to approach him, to subject herself again and again to his filthy gaze and wandering hands. She always manages to get away from him before anything really bad happens, but she sleeps badly and has troubled dreams that she's alone and he sees her, comes close, smiles, takes out his penis. She wakes up with a start, body taut with pleasure and hatred.

No more parties, she decides.

She keeps looking for an explanation for the jellyfish. Depending on the day, she tells herself they're because of the accident she had at fifteen, which propelled her from the carefree mindset of a happy life to consciousness of her own mortality—or maybe they're just the necessary sufferings of her journey toward full awareness. Or maybe it's just the narrow-ness and confinement of bourgeois life and the terrible vacu-ousness of social role-playing, of the masks we wear. There are certainly enough unacknowledged skeletons in triple-locked closets in her own family. She searches. She attends endless group therapy sessions and individual sessions and vocal yoga sessions. She stops buying pot. She wants to understand, she wants to move forward; the desire to live thunders inside her and throws her into terrifying rages she can barely conceal beneath conventional cool politeness.

In her individual therapy sessions she is often tripped up by the same hurdle: she is sad and discouraged; she breathes deeply, sinking into her own feelings, and suddenly anger burns fiercely in her throat; her mouth opens wide in a silent scream; she chokes, and very quickly she is no longer sitting there in the office with its egg-carton-covered walls, but small and lost and frozen, standing in the middle of a vast white expanse, waiting.

She calls this place *my little girl on the ice floe*. She doesn't yet know how very much longer that little girl will have to wait for me to come.

She is twenty-three years old. She starts writing the story of *Jeanne, the girl with gypsum-colored eyes*. She thinks about it a lot but writes very little.

She lands a small role on a popular network detective series, and one day, which began very early in the morning, she is resting alone in a trailer, curled up in one of the comfortable make-up chairs, when one of the lead actors enters. She pretends to be asleep; she doesn't like the intentness of his gaze or his repeated remarks about her ass (he calls her his *white black girl*). He comes closer. She keeps still, eyes closed, and then, suddenly, a thick-lipped mouth presses against hers. She is paralyzed. He gives a deep boom of laughter and leaves without saying a word.

That spring she falls passionately in love with a gifted, green-eyed guitarist. They are both as awkward as they are affected by one another, and she is soon spending almost every night at his place.

They make love, but at each penetration, he has to force his way inside her as she grits her teeth; the narrow orifice is always dry. Once he is in, though, she learns to relax, and sometimes experiences the delicious giddiness of a joint orgasm. As long as his fingers don't come anywhere near the joining of her thighs. As long as she's drunk enough, if he wants a blow job.

She reaches the end of her three years at ESAD and, the day after the public presentations, she wakes up nauseated. The compliments showered on her when she came offstage—*ravishing, beautiful, radiant*—make her want to vomit. She has no idea who this girl is that they're talking about.

She attends a wedding at the same place where she had her scooter accident eight years earlier. Nothing in her life since then has had the same rich beauty as that experience at the outermost frontier of her existence, so she clings to the sensations that kept her tethered to life that night: the explosive sweetness of biting into a crisp apple; the scent of pine needles rolled between her fingertips; the vibrant moistness of a handful of damp soil against her palm. She clings tightly to these, to keep from falling off a roof, tumbling out a window.

In the autumn she swaps her voice yoga classes for a course in the Feldenkrais Method, to which she was introduced the previous year.

One day the teacher is absent, and a substitute replaces her. She studies the bodies stretched out on the floor with the loving scrutiny an entomologist reserves for an unknown species of insect. She watches Adélaïde working, suggests a few movements, and then asks:

"Tell me, when I ask you to align your pelvis with the rest of your body, how do you do it?"

"I check it against the floorboards, or my two arms, stretched out straight."

"Okay. So, in fact, you use the floor, or your arms, to determine the position of your pelvis?"

"Yes; isn't that the right way to do it?"

"You're starting with the outside to understand an inner movement. Could you try to do it the other way around? Feel your pelvis from the inside, and adjust your position accordingly?"

For the rest of the class she tries and tries, but she just cannot manage to inhabit her own pelvis. She can feel her feet, her calves, her thighs, and then her stomach and chest and arms and skull, but there is a gap in the middle, an emptiness, a blank space where sensation ceases, to reappear further on.

She doesn't sleep that night, revisiting in her mind her theater instructors' comments, the perplexity of her boyfriends; the boredom she feels when she has to make love. She can't feel her own pelvis! She is living with a falsehood, a facsimile in which nothing can spark feeling. Her real pelvis has disappeared, and a long time ago too, probably, since it's never occurred to her that it could be any other way. She doesn't understand.

By day she goes about her business, passing her driving test and going to one casting call after another; by night she plunges into the effervescent scene of jazz clubs and concerts with her boyfriend. She needs, above all, to be distracted from herself.

Just after Christmas, more than two hundred thousand people are killed when a tsunami ravages the Indian Ocean. She gorges on the photos of swollen blue corpses that fill the newspapers, even as she hates herself for doing it.

A sixty-eighter stage director with a distracted, brilliant mind hires her to work on his next project. She has had television roles, but this is her first opportunity to act on the stage with professionals, and she is delirious with excitement. The actor playing her lover insists that they have to *go out for coffee together, and drinks, and get to know each other, so the onstage bond will be more realistic.* She believes him. He has more experience than she does. And he seems nice.

He flirts with her from the very first coffee in a café on the place Denfert-Rochereau. It bothers her; she feels obligated to slip in a pointed *I'm sorry, but I have a boyfriend*, and he answers, with a beguiling smile, *Now, why would you think you have to tell me that?* She feels like an idiot, vaguely guilty at the forced intimacy he has established.

The cast is tight-knit and welcoming, and she wants to become part of it. The others smile at her apparent bond with the leading man, exclaiming at how cute they are together, but his words stick and cling to her; she can hear them even after he's left the room. His hands wander and graze, every day more deliberately. She begins to suffer violent stomach cramps and bursts into tears on the metro without knowing why. She has filthy nightmares.

When the show opens, he forces a kiss on her behind the curtain just before she goes onstage. On set in the dim light, when the audience's attention is elsewhere, he lets his hand drift down the curve of her back and squeezes her ass; she can't move to shake him off.

One evening, he almost kills her in his car. He insists on driving her home; frighteningly drunk, he is so insistent that she doesn't dare refuse. He spends the whole drive emitting the piteous complaints of the lover rejected by the frigid bitch, while she shrinks into the passenger seat with every jerk of the steering wheel. The car ends up on a sidewalk between a bench and a plane tree.

She doesn't tell her boyfriend about it, or her therapist, or anyone else. She believes him when he reproaches her for being *repressed, cold, sexless*; when he insinuates that it's her fault, that she's the one torturing him, the one provoking him. There have been too many jellyfish inside her for too long for her to notice the new tentacles. Her stomach aches; she loses her voice; she agonizes before going onstage, but she doesn't see the connection. She's just being difficult, she thinks.

She consults a phoniatrician after her voice gives out for the umpteenth time: *Functional dysphonia with acute jaw tension.* They prescribe a set of exercises to be done twice a day. She never manages to finish even one; she has hardly begun moving her jaw when the jellyfish rise up, crushing her forehead and sending hot blood streaming down her face; raining blows on her body; slashing with scissors to widen her smile horribly. She slaps herself and the jellyfish surge backward. The phoniatrician reproaches her for not keeping up with her exercises, but how can she possibly explain? She cancels her follow-up appointments.

After the play closes, she fails casting call after casting call: too superficial, too jittery, too deliberate, too stiff. She writes in her sky-blue notebook: *How can you make yourself believe in yourself, all by yourself? The future is a blank slate and I'm afraid of sliding off of it.*

It would take me almost ten years to apply the terms *sexual harassment* and *sexual assault* to the stage actor's words and actions, and the kiss the TV star forced on me. Ten years to fully understand how disastrously harmful those first professional experiences were for me. Ten years to stop feeling like they were all my fault.

By the age of twenty-four she is going in a million different directions at once; she plunges into a thousand activities, stuffing her mind with projects. At night she dreams of running late; during the day, she makes sure never to be early. Never to leave any room for the jellyfish to creep in.

If a man's gaze skips over her without lingering, she is no longer sure that she exists. So she laughs, tosses her hair, plays the clown, talks about anything at all, as long as he pays attention to her, as long as she can see her jittery reflection in his eyes. Anything to hang on to the elusive feeling that she belongs to the land of the living, to the ordinary world, the intelligible one. The one that makes sense.

Her therapist talks about family constellations; he thinks the method might help her discover what is making *the little girl on the ice floe* have to wait so long. She signs up for a weekend course.

It's in the same place as the group therapy sessions. Twelve of them sit on mattresses in silence. After a quick survey of everyone's first names and emotional states, the first constellation begins. The therapists pose two or three succinct questions to the young man who has volunteered to start and invite him to choose, from the group's participants, people to represent his parents and grandparents. Then the chosen representatives, in their stockinged feet, position themselves gingerly on the beige carpet, searching for the place that feels best to them, paying careful attention to the feelings and images that arise inside them and between them. Little by little, step by step, under the astonished gaze of the constellation-maker, an old family history takes shape out of nothing. It's enthralling; there are incredible, unexpected developments, dizzying discoveries, intense emotions.

She raises her hand to be constellated, eager to discover, finally, the source of her terror. But the person who incarnates *What is making the little girl on the ice floe wait* horrifies all the representatives of her family without any of them being able to name it or seeming to recognize it. *The constellation can only show what the constellation-maker is able to discover. The information will come when you're ready to receive it*, the therapists say, soothingly.

She emerges from the weekend relieved. She has found a way to drag her history out into the light.

That summer she goes to Italy to study with a female director who is a follower of Jerzy Grotowski. They work their bodies and voices to the point of exhaustion, until they're too spent to hold on to anything or even desire anything; until, finally, something new and vibrant happens. She pushes herself as hard as she can but even the fatigue doesn't loosen her up; she still can't let down her guard. She can't differentiate between dramatic tension and muscular tension. When she works to relax her face the noose only tightens around her throat, stifling her emotions and slurring her diction. She feels as if she is sinking under her own weight.

She does a second class and then a third amid the splendid fig trees and valleys of the Tuscan countryside, trying to tear off with her bare hands the shackles she has forged so carefully to keep the jellyfish away.

She spends a few days alone in a private home, intending to work on the manuscript of *Jeanne*. She barely writes. She sleeps, she binges on food, and she masturbates with brutal self-loathing.

When, later, on a train, her boyfriend observes reproach fully that she's gained more weight, she slaps him.

This year she has trouble making ends meet with her sporadic theater and television jobs, so she does some voiceover work for an American pornographic show. Young cameramen go into student keg parties and manipulate the drunkest young women, who, in return for a T-shirt or a baseball cap, start by flashing their breasts at the camera and end up masturbating, alone or in groups, in a tour bus transformed into a studio. She has to imitate their *Oh*s and *Ah*s, make their groans of *My God Oh Ah Oh my God Yes* understandable to a French audience. Her mind stores up hundreds of images of pink vulvas, brown vulvas, shaved and marketed vulvas, vulvas as if detached from the bodies of these young women who are mass-produced, all of them resembling one another, uttering the same cries in the same positions, molding themselves to adhere to whatever the cameraman wants from them, silencing their own sensuality, their wildness, their romanticism, believing themselves to be liberated when really they're only being exploited.

She's neither revolted nor shocked; she is like them. Their muddled, squalid, self-contradictory desires match her own.

She makes a New Year's resolution: *Take control of my fear so I can finally come face to face with the Monster.*

And, a bit later: *I'm so sad. If only I could at least know why.*

On the nights she sleeps alone, she often has the same awful dream. She's standing in the shadows, and suddenly she smells a strange odor, damp and sickening. Little by little her eyes adjust to the darkness, and she can see the walls of the small room she's standing in the center of; they're irregular, lumpy and asymmetrical, and they're moving. Four blank walls, a floor, a ceiling. The walls are striated with red muscle and covered with flesh. They're pulsating. *Lub-dub, lub-dub*. She knows that rhythm. *Lub-dub, lub-dub*—it's on the tip of her tongue—*lub-dub, lub-dub*—what is it, again? And it's her own heart lying there, in her hands, her bony, white hands; the walls are made out of her own flesh, and the skeleton standing tenaciously in the center of the room is her too, and the skeleton starts jumping and leaping, and hurling itself against the walls, and its pointy bones slash long ribbons of blood into the flesh of the walls, and thick jets of viscous white liquid that ooze and mingle together, and the room gets smaller and smaller, and the more blood and fat there is, the harder she struggles to breathe, the more she suffocates. And then she wakes up, drenched in sweat.

In therapy, she explores paths that comfort her for a while but always end up being dead ends. The binges, the sadness, the cruelty never disappear for long; a few days, maybe; sometimes a week or two. Her life is a dotted line. So much clawing at the paint on locked doors, rummaging through attics, hunting for some unknown source of pain makes her simmer with anger at her sisters, her brother, her parents, her grandparents, and every ancestor that came before them.

She participates in four more family constellation weekends; she tries holotropic breathing, rebirth, primal screaming, kinesiology, floral extracts, and St. John's Wort. She consults an etiopath and makes an appointment with an astrologist. She reads countless books on personal development, Indian spirituality, and nonviolent communication; she studies Jung and Schopenhauer. She's like one of those trick birthday candles that relight themselves endlessly until you drown them in a glass of water. She is the granddaughter of a legionnaire, and as long as there is a war on, she will return again and again to the front line.

She is twenty-five years old, and she can see her life stretching out in front of her, unrolling like a carpet, sweeping away into the future like the flip side of yesterday, always dragging her body along behind it, leaving a red, sticky trail.

She continues to work doggedly on the story of *Jeanne*. Sometimes she has barely begun writing when she stumbles over a word, which she then lingers on and studies meticulously, turning it over and over in her mind, contemplating every nuance and facet; but the words always seem to be one step ahead of her. There is always one she hasn't considered that unsettles her and takes her somewhere else; a vowel that sounds a bit too light, rhymes that don't work, a serendipitous turn of phrase, and she gets bogged down in a few sentences. Sometimes she stops writing without realizing it, and slides down and, with all the weight of her aged body, she sinks into dark water. Then she shakes herself, goes into the bathroom, splashes cold water on her face. Stares at herself in the mirror for a long time, unseeingly. And then there are only a few more hours to kill before the day ends.

At casting calls she is a caricature of herself. She blushes, babbles, trips over her own feet. She hardly thinks beyond the day after tomorrow; she can't bring herself to make even the shortest phone call or seek out work in any kind of active way. She is either above it or below it. She is upside down.

At one failed audition, when someone gives her the name of an acting teacher at the École de Jeu, she signs up for a three-day course.

There are a dozen participants, in comfortable clothes and bare feet, everyone as gracious and kind as they are starving for realness. After a gentle, careful warm-up of each part of the body, they spread out around the room and, as soon as everyone feels ready, a song begins. The assigned task is to let their bodies express freely whatever they feel moved to express, right there and then; to give themselves fully to this voice, these words, this music. She dances and leaps and exults; she collapses and starts again. She radiates a kind of mad energy; she is pleased, but the teacher quickly points out, *You're fooling yourself. You're pretending to be overwhelmed, but really you're only making things up. You're not showing anything, not letting yourself feel deeply. When you're this determined to conceal part of yourself, nothing truly gets through except the desire to hide.* A direct hit. Finally, a free port where she can let down her defenses and relearn the craft of acting. Finally, someone she can't bluff, who won't let her get away with cheating anymore.

She spends three years at the École de Jeu. Enough time to dismantle the walls she has built around herself, brick by brick; to strip herself bare; to want too much; to lose hope; to give up; to start over; to work hard; and finally to surrender herself. Enough time so that she no longer recognizes herself. Enough time to get to know herself.

Night by night, her wonderful love life with the sweet guitarist crumbles to bits. She feels alone. They still love each other as much as ever, but neither of them knows how to interpret the other's silences, overly preoccupied as they both are with the voids inside themselves. She stops feeling the desire of the early days. Mostly she just lets him penetrate her, because he wants to, because she owes it to him, because they're a couple.

With her friends, she clings to her smile like a drowning person to a life raft, and a few hours spent being the same as everyone else fills her with fierce joy every time. People outside her circle of close friends think she's a drama queen, always overacting the role of herself; they complain that she talks too loudly and laughs too hard and gets angry too quickly, and it's true that in public she can't stand still; she darts around and spins and jumps, and never, *never* stays on the same floorboard for too long.

Twice a week, at the École de Jeu, she works on unlearning her habits, on not being false, on paying attention to what feels most right inside her. She battles with her own blockages: the fucking pelvis that freezes up for nothing, the lump in her throat that thickens her voice, the vacuous smile that hijacks her mouth. Some days, her jaws hurt so much that she can't chew, so she drags her friends to an Indian restaurant for dhal, or surreptitiously cuts her food into tiny pieces.

During the rest of the week she works feverishly. Some evenings she wishes she could just start walking and keep going until she falls asleep propped against a tree stump somewhere, exhausted. When she wakes up a man would be there, and he'd say *Get up and walk*, his finger pointing in a specific direction, and she would get up and finally know the right way to go. Or maybe she could just bury herself in the ground, and rot along with the last autumn leaves.

As Christmas approaches, she and her boyfriend go backpacking in southern India.

In Thanjavur, they go to the Brihadesvara Temple. It's

very early, and the huge ochre granite building towers against the red sky, bare at this hour of swarming tourists, worshipers, and beggars. They're almost the only people there. Something inside her stretches or relaxes, the claw that digs stubbornly into the dust while the body rises; the step that weighs her down and makes her as heavy as an eighty-one ton stone, at the top of the temple, the keystone of the sky all around her. They pass countless statues of Shiva dancing in the first caressing rays of the rising sun. They take off their sandals and enter the sanctuary to participate in *puja*. She's been ambivalent about these rituals up to now, but this morning, as they await the prayers, she trembles with anticipation. They wait for a long time, sitting a few meters from the iridescent curtain concealing the deity, unable to discern what's happening on the other side beyond clinking and rustling and whispering voices. Finally, the curtain rises to reveal an enormous *lingam* of black stone, standing on top of a broad *yoni*. Brahmins with bare torsos are perched on a balcony to reach it; they stretch their arms out to pour basins of clear water over it, and milk, and melted butter. The liquids trickle in rivulets down the immense damp stone, mingling and spreading in the *yoni*. The curtain falls.

She sits, unmoving, dumbstruck. She can't get over what she has just seen. Two enormous genitalia: one, erect, streaming with come, inside the other. A newborn gleaming with amniotic fluid, springing forth from the womb. Creation; even Beauty. Absolute, intimidating, raw. At this moment, she belongs to something immense, something she can't define.

She tours the rest of the temple, silent, trembling, wanting; transfixed by the acrobatic statues, small and delicate, entwined and interlocked, gripping each other's hips, caressing one another, breasts and genitals erect, tongues busily at work, for eternity.

In her churches, the statues swoon only with sorrow and

affliction, and though there are naked women atop the capitals, they have a devil's forked tail on their asses. In her language, people sometimes make love, but mostly, men conquer, take, possess, penetrate, pound, screw, smash, and take apart women. They shoot their loads on them and make them dirty. In her country, frozen scenes in chic magazines eroticize pain and humiliation, and when people talk about liberated women living free, unfettered sexual lives, those women are usually tied to headboards, extolling the benefits for the skin of having a man ejaculate onto your face.

Today is the day she realizes that she has experienced only a pale ghost of her own sexuality, fearful and confused, disfigured by shame and devoured by guilt, where others celebrate the Joy of being alive in the intertwining of their bodies.

She is about to turn twenty-six, and she would really like to spend less time thinking about the circumference of her own ass and her own crass mediocrity. She wants so much to be wrapped in someone's arms and has so much difficulty asking for it.

Day after day, at the École de Jeu, she trips over the safety net she has woven so carefully to protect herself from the jellyfish. She tries and tries to feel something she hasn't constructed or invented herself, some true, raw emotion, but whenever she gets too close to herself, she freezes, leaves her body, withdraws, avoids, pretends.

On one ordinary afternoon, with no warning, she is working to music, trying to feel her pelvis when the jellyfish rise up, coming from every direction, squeezing her and crushing her, their tentacles filling her mouth until she can't breathe. She is suffocating. She collapses to the floor, which gives way beneath her. She panics. She's going to die of fear; die for real, this time. The teacher grabs hold of her. *Look at me! Look at me, Adélaïde; come back to us! Stop telling yourself stories that aren't true; this isn't real!* She clings desperately to that face, that voice. She calms down slowly, pulls herself together, and opens her eyes, gasping, dazed; she has no real idea of what just happened. She tries to convince herself that this is just another story she's telling herself, a horror story, and goes on with her work . . . and yet. This Horror that just reached out and grasped her, she knows, was no invention; it is too monstrously familiar to her. It comes from somewhere, from a dark and bottomless pit carpeted with polyps, from the very depths.

On another afternoon she goes to the movies with her boyfriend. The end credits are rolling when the vice suddenly clamps down on her throat. She chokes, unable to catch her breath. She wrenches herself out of the chair; she has to get out of there. She collides with walls and people; *Get out of my way!* She falls to her knees on the sidewalk outside the theater, her hands pressed to her mouth. Her boyfriend panics and screams, *Calm the fuck down*, smashing his fist into a pole. Silence. One blow is enough to turn her back into the nice, guilty girl who is so sorry and so much easier to live with. For him.

Another time, a time like so many others, she has a sudden attack in the middle of the street and there are no churches or bathrooms nearby, no enclosed space where she can pull herself together, but she can't go another step further. She slaps herself with all the strength she can muster, trying to shock herself back to the present, to catch her breath. She clings to the doorjamb of a building, suffocating, slipping. She is horribly sick; she's going to die, facedown on a stone step that stinks of piss. Then, little by little, like always, it passes. She stands up, runs her fingers through her hair, passes her hands over her face, and resumes her place in the crowd of pedestrians.

She hears about a kind of physical therapy that uses touch and decides to give it a try. Session after session, she lies on a massage table in her underwear, and under the precise hands of a kind woman she learns to tense or relax more and more specific areas of her body, to sense the emotional climate that occurs inside her when she immobilizes them. She sets two goals for herself: to find her pelvis, and to break her habit of trying desperately to seduce every man that passes by.

In early summer, at a psychotherapy session, she is particularly despondent. She concentrates and sinks, sensation after sensation, burning throat, hollow chest, knotted stomach. She goes further down, and there is nothing—but wait, yes, there is. The little girl on the ice floe, waiting. As usual.

> she twists curls into herself a hand clamped
> over her mouth another on her genitals
> *he's rubbing me there*

She has no idea who or where; no context, nothing but the horror of a large male hand on her small child's vulva and the phrase

> *This will do you good.*

She feels so small, so defenseless. She pushes away the theory of the man from the stairwell, the May man. What he did wasn't so bad, in her recollection; yes, he put his hand down her underpants—but she doesn't remember being so terrified, so nauseated; she doesn't remember feeling anything at all. It was only *touching*.

Day and night, she reviews her memories of every man from her childhood. She doesn't tell the guitarist about it; she keeps her fake smile firmly in place. She buries the Horror deep inside herself.

Later she joins him in Majorca, where he is rehearsing with his jazz group. She's bought a bunch of pretty dresses in anticipation of a salvage-and-seduction operation that takes a nosedive under the stars on the very first night. They haven't even begun their romantic dinner when he breaks up with her. They eat anyway, and walk on the beach, and talk, and cry.

She spends the rest of the summer party-hopping and living on alcohol. She would love to devour every man she sees, to fill the emptiness, to have company on the ice floe, but her suffering is too obvious to make her attractive to anyone. She loses thirteen pounds in a month.

She forsakes the snug cocoon of the family home and gets her own place on her return to Paris. Each week she spends two days at the École de Jeu; an hour in psychotherapy; and another hour in physical therapy. She participates in three new family constellation weekends and a class on the issue of self-perception. She consults an energy healer, tries Bach flowers, has her aura cleansed by correspondence. She searches, and fights.

On the night before her twenty-seventh birthday, she writes: *I don't understand the journey I'm on, but I want to finally look like myself, like that photo taken while I was sleeping, with a thousand unknown shadows dancing on my face. Maybe even this path, whose edges are becoming clearer, less confused, is yet another mirage. But I've come too far to go back now, and even if this road is uncertain, even if the fog only retreats a few centimeters each time, it's still the path I've chosen, and I've dug its furrows with my own tears, my doubts, my rage, and my insatiable curiosity.*

During the physical therapy sessions, as soon as she tries to tense or relax her inner thighs, her lower abdomen, or her perineum, she becomes nauseated, acid rising in her throat. The practitioner asks her if she's ever been a victim of sexual violence, so she confides in her about being *touched* by the man in the stairwell one Sunday in May, and also about the other memory, the one that came back to her in therapy last year, the large male hand on her small vulva—but whose hand, and when, she still can't remember.

A few months later, during a session, working endlessly on her feelings on disgust, her body suddenly contorts

between the thighs
a big rough hand thumping her vulva thumping
brutal fingers forcing going inside
the bruising of a fingernail on her vaginal wall

he's inside me he put his fingers inside it's him

Terror, hate, violence, contempt, disgust
pain, power, perverseness.
All mixed. All mingled.

She's in the stairwell of her building. Everything is unchanged, like in the bedroom of a dead child, with the doll still posed carefully on the pillow and the markers uncapped on the little desk.

She spends the next week and a half in bed beneath the covers, in pieces, feigning a bad case of the flu so no one will suspect anything. She congratulates herself on having moved out of her parents' house and is relieved to be single.

After that session she can feel fingers inside her a thousand times a day, every day. The impression of a moist cock seems branded into her palm. Discreetly, so no one will notice, she bites her lips and the insides of her cheeks, pinches herself, digs her fingernails into the soft pads of her fingers, pulls out her eyebrow hairs, wipes her hand on her pants. She has to drive out the burning on the lips of her vagina and the filthy wetness in the palm of her hand. She doesn't stop chatting, working, laughing. She makes do.

One director says to her, *You're shrinking; you're too childish; you're basing your persona on your inner child. You need to be more rooted in your sexuality.* But what *is* her sexuality? A couple of days ago she gave a blow job to a male friend, spit the semen into the sink, brushed her teeth, and went home. Then, she binged on food. She plays the role of a libertine woman, and then fills her mouth with more gnocchi than it can hold. She hates blow jobs. She hates the smell of men's penises and getting too close to them makes her stomach turn. If a man presses her head to his crotch, she wants to kill him—and then she floats out of her body, leaving only the acquiescent doll. The only solitary pleasures she understands are filthy ones, degrading and debasing herself in the secrecy of bathrooms. Yet she would love to be the red-headed vamp in reality; the buxom, liberated woman some see in her. She would love to experience a sexuality that is joyous and simple and mutual, but she can't manage it; she is, depending on the day, the timid virgin, the sexpot, the frigid woman, the nymphomaniac, the submissive damsel, the whore, the Madonna. She knows full well that none of the stereotypes she puts on and sheds are really her. She has no idea what a *woman* really is, or what *female sexuality* really means; she is a woman in a civilization created by men, and she can see her own sexuality only through the lens of theirs.

She falls in love practically every month. Like Sleeping Beauty, she hopes each kiss will be the one to wake her up, to heal her, and every new man is Prince Charming for a few days or a couple of weeks. She is dazzled, swooning, *Oh my darling never before you never have I felt so strongly*, and the jellyfish disappear. But she is so enthralled and passionate in their arms that it overwhelms them. They feel burdened, and they run. Or they return her fascination, and she breaks their hearts as soon as the initial charm wears off, sinking back into her usual hateful lethargy, until the next pair of lips comes along.

In the spring she starts writing a novel set during the Liberation. A young woman's head is shaved, she is in love, he's German.

She is twenty-eight years old. If she waits until she's better to start writing, she tells herself, she'll never start writing at all.

She begins a friendship with a man she met on set a couple of jobs ago. He is fascinating, sixtyish, and it takes some time before she realizes what he is after, deep down: a fuck. It's the same old tune as with every guy in her profession: *You're wonderful, you have real talent; I'm going to help you get your big break*, and then their hand between your thighs. She's heard it many times, too many; she's had enough of their conditional promises, enough of swatting their hands away, enough of it being up to her to apologize, every time.

She has been seeing a new nutritionist and her diet improves, but though the times between binges grow slightly longer, the constant worry about eating or not eating weighs her down. She decides to devote her sixteenth day of family constellation therapy to the issue of bulimia. The morning afterward, something incredible happens halfway through her bowl of cereal: she is no longer hungry. She can't remember ever feeling this before; a sense of satiety, the delicate satisfaction of stopping when you've had enough.

Meal by meal, she discovers a love of good food; the

exquisite pleasure of savoring a dish slowly, anticipating it in advance, enjoying the flavors, letting the aromas blossom in her mouth without chasing them away too quickly with another forkful. She also learns, soon enough, that her new-found gourmandise is systematically accompanied by searing pain in her jaw. She makes do.

In early summer, at a wedding where she knows absolutely nobody and at which she was convinced she'd be bored stiff, she meets a tall guy with whom she falls instantly in love. She is awed at the intensity of the emotion, and by this sensitive, funny man who seems to feel the same way as she does. He is ten years older than she is, he warns her, and has two children, and it's high time he saw a psychiatrist. Their courtship is chivalrous and old-fashioned; it's two months before they even kiss. She's a long way from her lightning-fast conquests and disposable men.

As the months pass, their love carries her along, and any-thing seems possible, now. She is hired for four performances by very different directors whose artistic visions and intentions she loves; she travels, accumulating research and ideas for her novel; she tries her hand at slam poetry. She wishes she could force all the stories waiting and gathering dust inside her to come bursting out.

So yes, there are still unexplained anxiety attacks; still the burning between her legs a thousand times a day; the constant surveillance of herself and her surroundings, the overwhelm-ing temptation to hit herself, the frequent lapses of attention in the middle of conversations, the exhausting need to be noticed by men, the pain in her jaws. But she encourages her-self; she looks to the future, envisioning the day after tomor-row, and, onstage, she allows herself to experience both texts and characters fully and completely. She often feels happy. She is proud of all the work she has done to come this far.

She feels like she is finally starting to get better.

The historical research for her novel is finished; the first chapters have taken shape, and with every paragraph she becomes more afraid. As soon as she starts writing her head spins, and the words slip through her fingers; she can't retain them, and soon she won't be able to find them at all, and she'll be stuck there, silenced, waiting, on the ice floe. By judging herself too much, censoring herself too much, she grinds up each sentence until she has written nothing but a heap of dust.

One day when she is at rehearsal, someone comes in through the unlocked doors of the theater and steals her laptop, and with it her research notes and the first snippets of her novel, as well as rough sketches for other novels, the manuscript of *Jeanne*, short stories, poems, and stray pieces of text. None of it has been backed up or printed or e-mailed; she's never let another soul read it. The jellyfish unfurl their umbrellas wide and let their silky tentacles dance in the icy waters. After that, whenever she sits down to write, she can feel them massing in her gut; after only a few words they rush in, piling up inside her, rising into her throat, suffocating her. She is afraid they'll spill out of her mouth and blot out the horizon forever. She stops writing.

For several years now she has been sharing her love of reading, her joy in telling stories, with disadvantaged children.

She loves it—helping, sharing—but she wants a more political sort of involvement, so she joins a feminist acting troupe that organizes workshops for male-female equality. As part of her training she attends a symposium on sexual violence. She is shocked by what she learns—and shocked, too, that she is hearing all of it for the first time. She takes eighteen pages of notes.

The traumatic impact of violence is dependent on the victim's confrontation of the destructive intentionality of her abuser, and absolutely not on her own personality, nor even on the facts, strictly speaking!

All abusers use the same grooming strategies to isolate their victims and compel them to silence, in order to ensure their own impunity!

One captivating psychiatrist who specializes in caring for victims of sexual violence gives a masterful explanation of how the brain short-circuits during a rape, how a buried traumatic memory of the event is created, and the devastating consequences of this on the victim's health, sexuality, and social life.

She notes down the terms *dissociation, high-risk behavior, avoidant behavior, panic attacks, reluctant self-inflicted violence, repetitive nightmares, sensations of penetration.* Victims understand none of these symptoms, she writes. *The younger the victim when attacked, the more acutely she suffers from amnesia and post-traumatic stress disorder, and the less able she is to see the connection between present panic attacks and past assault.*

She writes all these things down avidly, but she isn't able to see the connection either.

On her thirtieth birthday, a girlfriend takes her to a café where they do free tarot card readings, as long as you arrive early and wait a long time. She's told to think of a question that she holds very close to her heart. She asks, *What's holding me back from writing?*

When it's her turn, the tarot reader (flanked by three students who nod every time he speaks) looks at her closely, lays down several cards, asks a few questions, and offers up a diagnosis: as long as she is, in her mother's mind, the reincarnation of her grandfather, she won't be able to have her own life. He prescribes a *psycho-magic act*: she must enlarge a photo of her maternal grandfather's face, the hero of the family, and make a mask out of it. Then she must dress as a legionnaire, put on the mask and a traditional white, flat-topped military cap, and surprise her mother while wearing the disguise, announcing, *I am your father.* Then: *Take off this mask and undress me*; and, once completely nude: *I am your daughter, and this is the first time you're seeing me.* Next she must get dressed again, but in women's clothes this time, a lacy dress and high heels. Then she and her mother must tear up the photo-mask together, dig a hole in the ground and bury the fragments, and plant a green plant on top of them. This, the man insists, is the only way she will be able to write and finally to have her own life, a life that will now be *stimulating and luminous.* She wants to burst out laughing, but everyone is looking at her so gravely. She shivers; she is utterly lost. The tarot reader seizes her hand. *If you want to be fulfilled, if you want to write, you must do exactly as I've told you; it's the only way for you. Once an act has been ordained, it must be carried out.*

I didn't do it. I didn't turn up in my parents' elegant living room disguised as a hero of the Resistance and talking like Darth Vader. My legionnaire grandfather, who was killed in Indochina a few months before my mother was born—I'd already exhumed him a thousand times in therapy; I'd sounded the depth of each impact again and again, just like I'd conducted detailed autopsies of so many cadavers, rummaged through so many closets, hammered out so many issues. I wanted to understand what I had, what was wrong with me, and I wouldn't rest until I did, and he undoubtedly sensed it, that tarot-reading crap-artist who wanted me to believe that my whole life depended on a ridiculous vaudeville act.

Soon afterward, she moves with her boyfriend into an apartment large enough for the two children of whom he shares custody, and she ventures out onto the shifting sands of being a stepmother. She can't believe her luck, this wonderfully attentive and gentle man, the sudden, disconcerting simplicity of loving and being loved.

That autumn, during a week of training with the feminist acting troupe, one afternoon is dedicated to the penal framework of violence against women. It's teatime; cakes and sugar-packets littering the table, everyone noting conscientiously on their memo pads that *psychological harassment, sexual harassment, and sexual assault are misdemeanors in France, and referred to as such by the district court and its three judges, but rape, murder, and torture are felonies judged in circuit court, by three judges and six jurors selected at random.* The director reads from some articles of the law: *Any act of sexual penetration, of any nature whatsoever, committed against the person of another individual by means of violence, coercion, threat, or surprise, is a rape.* She defines each of the terms: *Penetration can refer equally to forced fellatio, vaginal fingering, or*

vaginal fingering?

The words are like thunderbolts.

What she has, for more than twenty years, called *sexual touching*—his fingers inside her then, his fingers inside her remembered four years ago and every day since, was a RAPE. Maybe she isn't so crazy after all; maybe there is a reason for her suffering. Someone did something bad to her; someone did that word to her. Rape. What if that word is the key she's been looking for all this time; all these years of searching in vain?

II

She's thirty-one years old. She's moving forward, doing better, but every time she manages to live in the here and now even for a moment, exhaustion descends on her like a lead weight; days of bleakness and prostration inevitably follow on the heels of both breakthroughs and happy times.

One day she tells her psychotherapist about the violent visions in which she sees herself dead on every street corner, crushed, dismembered, eviscerated, several times a day, every day. *It's nothing really serious, but now that I'm riding a bike in Paris it's annoying; it makes me lose my concentration.* He is shocked. Why hasn't she ever told him about this in almost ten years of therapy? Now she's the one taken aback. *I'm so used to it; I don't even pay attention to it.* She smiles sheepishly. *I didn't think it was worth mentioning. No, I don't know exactly when it started. Even as a teenager I had trouble concentrating; these images would crop up all the time. But really, it's not that bad. It's just when I'm on my bike that it bothers me.*

There are so many horrors she doesn't tell him about. It doesn't even occur to her to tell him about them.

With the feminist acting troupe, she leads workshops in writing and drama in high schools in Île-de-France. Spending a lot of time on public transportation, she rediscovers the tricks she used when she was younger: wearing a scarf to discourage men from staring at her chest; standing with her backside pressed to the doors to avoid rush hour wandering hands;

keeping her head and eyes down; reading a book or fixing her gaze on her phone; looking unavailable. She's lost count of the exhibitionists, street harassers, and gropers encountered during her years as a city dweller; the guys in cars who slow down and ask for directions with their cocks exposed; the ones who sit down directly across from her on the metro and masturbate so only she can see it; the ones who describe exactly how they would fuck her, and how they get a hard-on thinking about her pussy; the ones who insult her mother's and grandmother's sexuality because she won't give them her phone number; the ones who—she's all too familiar with the impunity of men in public spaces.

One evening at the Luxembourg RER station, a group of fifteen or so middle-class guys in kilts get on the train. They're celebrating the outcome of a rugby match with shots of alcohol and obscene songs extolling rape and physical violence against women. They're extremely pleased with themselves, shouting out the words with such brutality that she curls into herself and covers her ears. She wishes all the women in the carriage would stand up with her and order them to stop, but she can't even manage to raise her head. One of them, an up-and-coming young executive by the look of it, his shirt crisply ironed, and glasses crooked, gets uncomfortably close to her and drunkenly spits out the lyrics from some filthy French doggerel about a man ass-raping a woman while she's asleep and claiming she loved it.

La digue du cul non ce n'est pas le diable
Mais mon gros dard poilu, la digue du cul . . .

No one intervenes. She flees the train at the next station, running, sobbing. She has had more than enough of these men who measure their dicks by the amount of fear they cause.

In her workshops, she helps young people who, in exercise after exercise, sort through and distinguish between words that designate and words that judge; those that are clear-cut and objective, and those we impose on ourselves. She witnesses breakthroughs by resigned young girls who suddenly flush purple when they realize how they have allowed themselves to be subjugated. She learns to recognize victims' symptoms; to establish the kind of trust that allows painful words to be spoken and crimes to be disclosed, often for the very first time. She learns how to turn the follow-up and aftercare over to skilled professionals, how to report misdemeanors, felonies and harm, and how to direct the victims' devastated companions to trustworthy organizations. In the course of these workshops, the words she has learned in training—*sexism, homophobia, spousal abuse, child witnesses/victims, child-rearing violence, incest, female circumcision, forced marriage, polygamy, sexual harassment, sexual abuse, rape, gang rape*—these words, all of them become the stories of the terrific girls and boys who make her heart overflow with love every time she sees them; brave young women and men with brilliant smiles and horrifying pasts. And at their trembling, accusing words, she feels the shame fading and the anger rising inside herself, her head filling with ideas and her mouth with words too long left unsaid.

The timidity of the early days with her boyfriend has vanished, and they no longer need to drink alcohol before they make love. Sober, each time his penis is poised at her entrance she bites her lips, tensing and stiffening. She wants to be in the moment; she doesn't allow herself to be subsumed by disgust. She tries to ignore the fingers. She focuses on the face of the man she loves, and together they cross the fetid threshold. The bright passion returns. She has told him about it. She had to; he wondered who the bogeyman was that climbed into bed with them every time. He has learned to live with the *ménage à trois*.

They marry in early summer. She feels, finally, as if she is living in the same world as everyone else, and during the preparations for the wedding a bit of the long curtain she has drawn between herself and her family is torn away, that curtain behind which she always imagined them standing and smiling, grouped together apart from her, hands over their eyes and, on those hands, large cartoon eyes that looked at her without seeing her. But she, who never knew how to act lighthearted at the family dinner table, who made them recoil from her stubborn convictions and pointless arguments, who felt that she'd been labelled as oversensitive, overly delicate, intolerant; she, who could have been a success but instead prefers to teach workshops for underprivileged/etc. kids, the ingrate who complains even though she has everything—in the end she has judged them too, looked at them without seeing them. The curtain was opaque in both directions. Tears shine in her father's eyes when he praises her *tireless zest for living* and smilingly emphasizes her *strange taste for psychiatrists, which is a bit incongruous, perhaps, but after all, our ancestors had their vicars and confessions.* She realizes how incomprehensible, how hurtful, her rages and absences must have been when her older brother says, his tone subtly barbed: *It's not always easy to see it when you're the baby of the family, but you can ask around—you always got a lot of love; you were lucky enough to grow up in a loving household.*

She gets pregnant very quickly, and in her third month the jellyfish reappear and launch a vicious assault with no warning at all. She has horrific panic attacks from which she can't emerge without hitting herself, banging her head into walls, splashing her face with icy water.

She increases the frequency of her psychotherapy sessions; she's afraid her craziness will kill both her and the baby. And, during one session spent submerging herself in this fear, she finally manages to formulate a thought: *My uterus is my sanctuary; it's as if it was the only part of me that hadn't been soiled, which still belonged completely to me, so if a tiny penis is floating in it, that's the end of it; I have nothing that's just mine anymore, and I'll disappear.*

She doesn't know why she still feels so dirty, but the therapy sessions soothe her, and her husband is supportive. They have regular consultations with a wonderful midwife who practices haptonomy and gives good advice, and the jellyfish recede.

One winter evening when she is five months pregnant, she stops quickly at home on her way somewhere else. The landline rings, and she—who never picks up, because it's always patio or double-glazing salesmen—this time, she answers it.

"Hello, may I speak to Adélaïde Bon?"

"Speaking."

"Born in Paris on March 1st, 1981?"

"Yes, why?"

"Hello, ma'am, this is Captain Vidocq."

She bursts out laughing.

"This is no joke, ma'am. I'm from the Juvenile Protection Brigade."

"Oh, I'm sorry—I misunderstood; I thought my husband was playing a prank on me."

"Of course, that's all right. You filed a sexual assault claim in 1990, is that correct?"

"Uh—yes."

"Well, I'm calling to inform you that we've arrested a suspect in the case. I'm contacting you so that you can file a new claim."

He might have kept talking after that, but she can't remember it, can't process anything else. She's shaking, pressing her forehead, cheeks, hands to the window. She's burning up. She wants to laugh, to cry, to leap, to collapse. All these years and the police hadn't forgotten either; all these years, and the police hadn't abandoned her?

*

She calls her parents, her brother, her two sisters, her husband. She tells them that she's just been given the best Christmas present of her whole life. She sobs with happiness. *You're so sensitive it's ridiculous*, her oldest sister says. *It was such a long time ago.*

It's been twenty years and a bit since they last spoke about it. Twice now she's slipped the new word *rape* into conversations; once with her parents in the car, and once at a restaurant with her sisters. The second time, the younger one confided that when she was a teenager, a boy with whom she'd had a big summer romance had raped her. She hadn't said anything to anyone; how could she, at sixteen, find the words to describe what had, in a single instant and perhaps forever, destroyed love and trust and lightness? And who would have listened? Who would have believed her? It had taken her years, too, to label the catastrophe with the word *rape*.

Her sister. Her darling sister. They didn't embrace one another; they didn't dare. A few words in common weren't enough to undo years of reserve and solitude. When her sister added that a sex therapist she'd recently consulted had said that *that wasn't the reason she was suffering*, she was irritated, and retorted dryly that the sex therapist was clearly incompetent. She clammed up again after that.

Two months after the telephone call, she has a meeting at the Juvenile Protection Brigade to reiterate her deposition. She waits in a café for the preoccupied girlfriend who was supposed to help her prepare for the appointment, but arrives only in time to accompany her. The captain has asked for a photo of her at age nine, so she has two large school portraits in her bag. To distract herself from the fear and the waiting, she takes the photos out and places them side by side on the table. The first one, taken four months after the incident, features an impish little girl with laughing eyes and a nose sprinkled with freckles. The second one, taken a year after that, shows another child entirely; her eyes are dull, her cheeks drooping, her smile forced. Her dimples have disappeared beneath a layer of fat. She looks terribly sweet.

She stares at the impish little girl and doesn't recognize her. She strokes the photo with a fingertip, tracing the oval of the face; she doesn't dare touch the eyes, or the mouth. She trembles. The child looking back at her is a stranger.

She sits in the captain's office, clutching at her pregnant belly, at the new life growing inside her, at the kindly gaze of the police officer, at the details of the office, the armrests of her chair, the walls, afraid she will slip away. *You were the victim of a sexual assault in your apartment building. What do you remember?* the captain asks. She can't breathe.

It's the Sunday of the national school fair. I'm in fourth grade, or *huitième*, as they say in my affluent neighborhood in the sixteenth arrondissement. It's a beautiful, sunny day in May, and I'm wearing a round-necked white blouse under a pretty red polka-dotted jumper my mother sewed for me. My arms and legs are bare, and I have lacy white ankle socks and white sandals on.

That morning, after mass, I won a goldfish in a game of Knock-Down Cans. I brought it home triumphantly, holding it high in the air in its bag full of water and joy. My brother and my two sisters and my parents were all with me; we were hardly ever apart. During the week we had an *au pair* who went out with us.

In the afternoon I begged my mother to let me go back to school so I could buy fish flakes for my goldfish. Just this one time (what a joke, wasn't it, that it happened that time); just this once, Mommy, Daddy; I'm nine, I can go back by myself. I'm nine now, after all.

I got permission to go, and secretly bought three Carambars with the change. I felt a little guilty about that; I hoped the baby Jesus wouldn't come and give me a rap on the knuckles.

On the way back a man follows me, and asks me the time. I show him that my arms are bare, that I'm not wearing a watch. He has a sing-song voice; he asks me to stay there with him for a minute, but I tell him, *My mommy told me never to talk to strangers.* We've already reached my building, and he comes in too, *to get out of the sun.* He tells me he's supposed to deliver a bicycle to a girl, just the same height as me, just my size, who happens to live in the same building as me. He's nice. He's persuasive. I think the baby Jesus sent him so I can make amends for the naughtiness of the Carambars. He gets on the elevator with me and pushes a button. When we get to that floor, he grabs my wrist and makes me get off with him. It hurts. *Show me where the little girl lives; you're a nice girl.* I'm afraid. I climb the steps ahead of him, not daring to refuse, but everything already seems to be in slow-motion. He stops between two floors. *You're the same size, right?* Yes. *Then it'll be easier for me just to measure the height of the seat on you, rather than bothering them on a Sunday, won't it?* Yes. *You have to lift up your dress so I can measure you.* Okay. Or maybe I'd already stopped talking by then.

She forces herself to describe what happened next, but the fragments of memory aren't coherent. She can't remember if he or she lifted up her dress. *He put his hand in my underpants,* she says, but she doesn't think she was wearing underpants anymore by then. When did he pull them down?

I remember he had on a crocodile-skin belt with a gold buckle, she says, *which he unfastened when he took his penis out of his pants,* but she can't remember the penis itself.

She says, *He made me hold his penis in my hand. He made me move my hand on it.* The captain: *Caress it?* No, not at all; that's not caressing. But she must resign herself to perverting this word, for lack of a better one, for lack of a word that can encompass all the ugliness of the back-and-forth of a small child's hand on an adult's stiff penis.

She says, *He put his fingers inside me; I remember his finger wriggling inside me.* She doesn't dare use the word rape; she waits for him, the policeman, to say it. He writes everything down carefully, but he doesn't speak.

She says, *I was one stair above him. He was facing me.*

She says, *There was a noise downstairs, someone coming into the building, or maybe the concierge coming out of his office, and he stopped.* I know now that there was no noise downstairs. He didn't stop. She made that up about the noise, a long time ago, to protect herself from what happened next.

She says, *He took my hand and wiped it on his trousers.*

The captain compares her account with the one taken on the day it happened. She had said, *He went around behind me,* and now she has just said the opposite. *I don't know. He must have changed position.* When? She had said, *He touched my privates, in front and in back.* In back? She can't remember anymore. *He told me I had big thighs. He put his penis between my legs. I was really scared.* His penis between her legs? She can't remember anymore.

The captain asks her to describe him. She vividly recalls his pale blue short-sleeved shirt, his clinking crocodile-skin belt, his vaguely retro-looking grey canvas trousers; but she can't remember his penis or his hands or his eyes; she can't remember his gaze fixed on her, or the expression on his face. The memory is blurred, like the pixelated images on the TV news.

The captain shows her a sheet of photographs with four bald men staring back at her. Mug shots, taken from a man's height. Shadowed eyes, hard mouths. She hesitates. She isn't sure. It's been twenty-three years, and the face she remembers has holes instead of eyes. At nine years old she was barely four feet tall, and only saw him from below, in a low-angle shot.

The captain indicates one of the four sinister faces. It's the man from the stairwell, the May man, the one the police have nicknamed *the electrician*, a long-faced man, one Giovanni Costa. She hopes.

Over the next few days she finds some articles online that appeared in the newspapers the day after his arrest. *The man is active in the upscale neighborhoods of the capital; he usually claims to be an electrician needing help to reach a fuse box or a light bulb.*

She glances at the comments, which are mostly anonymous exchanges of insults. *Serves those rich assholes right*, exults one man. *I'm sure they must have cock-teased him, those little rich-bitch whores.* She sighs, thinking of the scathing e-mail sent a few months ago by an envious girlfriend: *What a hard time for poor, beautiful Adélaïde, born with a silver spoon in her mouth (oh, sorry, or was it a gold one?), who in spite of everything she has, still manages to complain and feel sorry for herself! Your childhood wasn't so bad; everyone loved you; you've got it all, and plenty of people have it a lot worse than you.*

Yes, of course that's true. Money might not have made me happy, but it's allowed me to pay for a psychotherapist all these years, and it's bought me the time I needed to try to get better. How lucky for me, to have been a *little rich-bitch whore*.

She is thirty-two years old and preparing as thoroughly as possible to deliver her baby, with the assistance of two midwives, one a haptonomist and the other a militant feminist who leads the birthing class magnificently. She is approaching the final month of her pregnancy when the panic attacks return with a vengeance. The closer her due date creeps, the more frantic she becomes. She is terrified that, at the moment of delivery, the fingers will slip inside her and steal away her baby.

One day she calls the feminist midwife in floods of tears after a new panic attack leaves her completely exhausted, and is given an appointment for the next day without having to say anything else. Then, her hand clutching her husband's, she tells the woman everything: the May man, the panic attacks, the fingers, the visceral fear that the baby will be soiled by passing through her private parts. She's terrified of the epidural; terrified of losing sensation in the pelvis she spent so many years trying to find; terrified that she'll leave her body and go blank at the crucial moment when her baby will need her most; terrified that the fingers will choke the newborn. Her husband admits his own distress and powerlessness. The midwife listens to them, reassures them, explains that these feelings of anxiety in late pregnancy are common in women who have been victims of sexual violence. She advises her to give birth without an epidural in order to maintain contact with the baby and with herself, and gives them invaluable advice on dealing with the pain. The haptonomist midwife will be in full agreement; coaching her husband to support his wife with his hands and to keep his eyes on hers, and reminding her to breathe, to sing with each contraction, to feel the baby inside her and help it descend the right way.

When the first pains begin on a magnificent, sunny day in May, she is confident; she is ready; she is present. Her voice accompanies each contraction with a deep, powerful chant, and the labor and delivery nurses stick their heads through the half-open door of her room to encourage this *bonze*-woman.

There is no trace of the man in the stairwell on this day, this glorious day, this beautiful May day, the day my son is born.

S he is a young mother, a great expanse of downy skin to cradle her newborn, with enormous ears wholly attuned to his breathing; she-wolf teeth to protect him from witches; lynx's eyes; huge, heavy breasts. In this loving and milky paradise, the jellyfish are hiding, readying themselves. The blank months have begun.

In the early autumn, death arrives unexpectedly for the psychotherapist who has been caring for her for eleven years. They had suspended their meetings for a few months, so she could focus on the baby; they were about to start the sessions again.

In a small country cemetery surrounded by green fields, she buries a friend, a mentor, a father. The safety harness is gone, and alone I will descend into the deepest and darkest of pits. He was the only person in the world with whom she felt no fear; the only one to whom she had ever dared describe some of her jellyfish, the only one to risk standing beside her on the ice floe. And now he is gone, and with him the little office nestled in the courtyard, the comforting islet where she could catch her breath. She drifts, and the jellyfish buffet her amidst the current.

She signs up for a writing workshop in the mezzanine of a feminist bookshop on the rue de Charonne, seeking a home port where she can offload a few of the jumbled phrases piling up vainly in her head. She's too afraid to write when she's alone.

After a few months she realizes, abashed, that no matter what assignment or scenario she is given, directly or indirectly she is always writing about that afternoon in May when she was nine, and about him, the man in the stairwell.

One Saturday they are instructed to start with an unspecified beginning chosen from among several. She doesn't hesitate; she knows immediately which one she will pick, even though she has never seen it before, even without knowing the book of which it is the opening phrase. She seizes it as one grasps a hand held out at the moment of falling, and she writes, all in one go, without lingering, without crossing anything out, without a single correction, this text:

"The morning I began this book,
I started coughing"
Like a thick coating which, from the violence of a single hiccup, finally begins to crack.

For as long as I can remember, I have put my hands to my throat when I'm emotional. I feel it, wrap my fingers around it, and calmness returns, and the storm subsides. My throat-vestibule, a decompression chamber between the inside and the outside, which allows me to arrange this amiable, smiling face, these laughing eyes, these charming dimples, this "be nice" no matter what.

On the pegs of my vocal cords I hang rage, hatred, disgust, contempt for myself and others, so my softened voice is dressed up in harmonious modulations. Don't let them see; don't let them hear. Let the storm batter against my diaphragm, my ribs; let the blizzard howl in my pelvis; do nothing to detach the talons piercing my aorta. Withdraw from this stupid and bleeding body.

My throat, a fireman's ladder to flee disaster, to run far away, to fly.

And yet, every morning when I wake up there is this awful taste of blood, this fierce, overwhelming desire to yawn, which would open my throat with forceps and enable me, finally, to vomit you out.

Because it's you; it's your law that reigns in my chest and governs my throat. Because since that day and those minutes outside myself, I have been yours. Or maybe you have been in me, because I don't know the difference anymore. I am your meal endlessly served, and nothing is left of me but the container, the goatskin your ghost drains to the dregs every day. And beneath my frozen, smiling face, the rage in my blood is all I have left of life. Of my own life. Of a life of my own.

And writing makes my heart pound so hard that I'm afraid my coughing will bring it up and it will spill on to the page.

And I imagine it, infected, pale, filled to bursting with pus and evil humors, and I'm afraid it will leap out and go wandering on its own, attack a passer-by and force its way into her throat, and the cough is back, and I am barking in the icy silence of this apartment. My hand grasps the words it writes, because only writing about you will give me back my voice, my own voice, a voice of my own. Once the book has gone to press I won't cough anymore. I will finally have other things to say.

Now she has to read. She hesitates, and in that hesitation, in that miniscule lapse of time before her decision to read aloud, she realizes that the time has come for her to write to be read. This will be her foundation text, the first words of many to come, the first thing I will share with a few friends, that I will read to a small group of strangers on the last day of my workshops, that I will send (unsuccessfully, by the way) to a contest.

On that day, the hand I grasped was Anaïs Nin's, and through the first words of her first book, *House of Incest*, she unquestionably came to my aid—through the mysterious sisterhood forged in an instant between her words and mine.

Since the phone call from the police—or, really, since the birth of her miracle baby, the jellyfish have changed, and the images are more terrifying than ever. Her days are full and happy—and then, without warning, they strike.

Capture the horror in words. Describe the blank months. My son, my beloved boy, my precious one might someday read these words. They will cause him pain, and I don't know if I will be able to fix it, to soothe away the pain of those words. But I'm going to write them anyway. I owe them to myself, and I owe them to the little girl waiting for me on the ice floe, and I owe them to all those living in pain.

                    at the movies a rape scene with torture
                        seatmates revolted, vagina engorged
                in the bath skin to skin with her newborn
                            imagining masturbating him
            wanting to rip her head from her shoulders
                            or drink a bottle of bleach
                            no longer able to breathe
                    the sick baby in the big bed at night
                        and his tiny bare feet so close
                                    to her genitals
                        trying to drown herself in the bath
            changing the baby's diaper his penis is hard
            imagining herself licking it with her tongue

wanting to sew her own eyelids shut
gripping the changing table
so she won't run to the balcony and jump
changing her tiny infant's diaper
and avoiding looking at his penis for fear of
changing the diaper and singing, telling a story
making jokes, above all above all filling in the gaps
a thousand times a day, gritting her teeth hard,
digging her fingernails deep into her skin
so the big fingers will withdraw from her vagina
secretly buying a vibrator to inflict
preventive violence on herself before she finds the baby
keeping from being alone at home keeping from being alone
with her baby boy keeping from thinking
keeping from thinking keeping from looking at
his little penis keeping from breathing too much keeping from

being lost

A day rarely goes by when she doesn't sink. When she's alone at home, she feels the large fingers inside her first, and then something else, something lurking, about to spring, that terrifies her. She's suffocating; she can't breathe, so, quickly, mechanically, she does what needs to be done for it all to stop: she goes and gets the vibrator, draws the curtains, pulls down her pants and underwear, searches Google for *porn video rape* (erotic novels, more erotic style of video stopped working for her a long time ago; they're not violent enough), and then degrades herself, defiles herself, abuses herself. In the dull throbbing of the blood vessels of her inflamed vulva, nothing is pleasant; nothing is gentle; nothing is restorative. She stares at the screen and she becomes the violence of the man throwing a woman to the floor and holding her by the back of the neck so she can suck him; she becomes the woman who controls her gagging to show that she likes it, that she could spend hours being penetrated that way, exposed, debased. After a time, whose length varies depending on the violence of the images and the intensity of the anxiety that preceded them, she stops, replete, ashamed, her vagina painful, her heart heavy. She is finally somewhere else. She spends the next few hours drifting, lethargic, nauseated, disturbed.

Eventually, one time doesn't calm her down for long enough, so she starts over again.

She finds it harder and harder to make love with her husband. He does everything he can to reassure her with tenderness and gentle words, but as soon as sex begins she is more afraid with every passing second, more fearful of the other one's fingers insinuating themselves between her thighs, and she is flooded with disgust and terror. She has to bite her tongue hard, dig her nails hard into the pads of her fingers, cling to her husband's loving gaze, when the other one is there. She is drowning.

One night they are kissing, entwined, and everything explodes. She shoves him away so hard that she falls backward off the bed, white-faced, tormented. The other one is there; she can feel his hands all over her and the sickening smell of his cock. She tries frantically with her small hands to wipe him off her skin, her mouth, her buttocks, her vagina. She is nauseated, eyes bulging, trying to vomit out her own tongue.

That night will come back to haunt every night from then on.

She confides some of it—the only part she can bear to put into words; the common, accepted fears and anxieties generally experienced by female victims—to a girlfriend, who contacts Dr. Salmona, the renowned psychiatrist whose presentation at the symposium several years ago made such a powerful impression on her.

The psychiatrist can't see her until the summer, when people's vacations will free up some space in her crowded agenda. In the meantime, she reads her book, *The Black Book of Sexual Violence:*

> Unable to fully take on board and comprehend the mechanisms at the root of the traumatic memory, the victim endures these reminiscences and, most often, adheres to them as psychic productions emanating from her own thought processes, which are particularly frightening.
>
> She feels terrified, in a state of panic, believing that she is dying, even though she is in no danger from anything.
>
> She feels suddenly depressed and completely hopeless, with the only prospect that of committing suicide and disappearing, even though everything is going well for her and she loves life.
>
> She feels guilty and ashamed of who she is; she feels as if she has no value, as if she is ugly, stupid, less than nothing, a piece of garbage ready for the scrap-heap, even though she does everything to the absolute best of her ability. She sees herself as monstrous, violent, perverse, capable of doing evil things, even though she wants only to love and be loved. She believes that she desires violent and degrading sexual acts, even though she yearns only for tenderness.

Her eyes burn; a lump rises in her throat. She wants to scream her joy at the moon. Her heart bursts into a thousand golden pieces. This whole, long paragraph—every word of it is *her.*

> The traumatic memory of violent acts and of the abuser colonize the victim, and are the source of confusion between her and the abuser; confusion which is responsible for feelings of shame and guilt, and which are accompanied by violent and perverse words, images, and emotions wrongly perceived to be her own, even though they originate from the abuser.
>
> The traumatic memory haunts them, dispossesses them, and

prevents them from being themselves; worse, it makes them believe that they have a sort of double or even triple identity: a normal person (which they are) and a worthless person who is afraid of everything; a guilty person of whom they are ashamed and who deserves death; a person who could become violent and perverse, who must constantly be controlled and suppressed.

In the time it took to rape me, the man in the stairwell insinuated himself between the folds of my brain; he let his hatred and perversity macerate in the antechamber of my memory, and day after day they have seeped into it, tainting every one of my thoughts, contaminating my whole life. An invisible invasion that nothing helped me to detect, or name, or understand.

Since that Sunday in May there have been twenty-four years of invasion by forced entry, every hour, every minute. Filthy thought after filthy thought, I have found myself buried alive, quivering, crushed beneath hatred of myself and the terror that people can see it, that people know. And, especially, the poisoned thought that has haunted me since the birth of my precious baby

I could destroy my own son

No. These filthy thoughts aren't mine. The filth belongs to him.

S hortly after her thirty-third birthday she makes an appointment with an attorney recommended by the European Association Against Violence Toward Women in the Workplace. She wants to have her charge reclassified, upgraded from *sexual touching* to *rape*. She feels the word is necessary. She also wants to file a civil suit demanding reparation in her own name; to be kept up to date with the legal proceedings, and to be able to attend every phase of the trial.

To reach the attorney's office, she has to walk up two flights of stairs covered with the same carpet as her parents' stairwell, carpet woven in shades of red and blue and green and hell, that long carpet found in so many Haussmannian buildings and that she avoids systematically when she's alone, preferring to take the elevator. Today she goes on foot, crushing the god-damned carpet beneath every step.

The attorney is soft-spoken and keen-eyed, her figure slender and resolute, a dimple in her nose. Questioning and answering, point by point, she shows her a route through the obstacle course of justice, explaining, *This case involves both rape and sexual assault, so the trial will take place in a circuit court, presided over by three judges and six jurors selected at random to judge each of the offenses. Proceedings in circuit court cases can be extremely lengthy,* she warns. *You're going to have to be patient.* Now that they are united for the same purpose, they start compiling a list of evidence to be gathered and actions to be taken.

She receives her first *Victim Notification*. Reading the names of the thirty-four other girls, she is stunned to discover that she knows two of them. One was at school with her; the other is the older sister of the girl who was her best friend when she was nine—her best friend, to whom she said nothing. You don't have the words to talk about something like that, when you're nine years old.

She likes her very much, the older sister. They were in an elective drama class together when she was a high-school sophomore and the other girl was a senior, both part of a small and tight-knit group. She finds her telephone number and calls her. And, like water rushing in the moment a gate is unlocked, they tell each other their stories. He used the same words with both of them, the same phrases. It's the same man. It's him, the man whose name may be Giovanni Costa. She hangs up, and curls into a ball on her big bed, and sobs.

There is another little girl living on the ice floe. I will never be alone again.

S ummer finally arrives, and with it her first session with the psychiatrist. Her office is nestled at the rear of a leafy courtyard filled with twittering birdsong and, in the waiting room, the words *me too* shine softly in some of the other faces. The doctor arrives; she apologizes for being late, guides her toward a cluttered office, invites her to be seated, sits down herself, looks at her.

She will tell this woman everything. Everything she has never dared to tell another soul; everything that fills her with so much shame, everything in her that is so abhorrent, so insane, so perverse. The psychiatrist diagnoses her with *post-traumatic stress disorder*.

As the sessions progress, in the course of explanations of brain function and traumatic memory, the jellyfish are transformed into symptoms, consequences, and the May man into a pedocriminal. She is relieved that she no longer has to use the enemy word, the lying word: *pedophile*.

The first time she relates all the facts, she starts with the sunny Sunday, the school fair, the goldfish, the Carambars, and the man who speaks so politely, who takes the elevator, who pulls her toward the staircase. Halfway through, she stops, confused. She can't remember any more of what happened next but a few incomplete fragments, always the same ones, as if she is seeing them from a great distance. Then she finds herself back at the top of the stairs, dressed again.

When? The fabric of the story is ripped. There is a hole torn in her history.

A month later, in the refuge of the office, she is trying to remember, and suddenly everything shifts.

> *I'm in the stairwell he is there he's looking at me*
> *he says words to me that I can't hear*
> *he does things to me that I can't feel*
> *he's looking at me*
> *his eyes are cold and metallic*
> *I don't exist in them*
> *I don't exist anymore*
> *I have just stopped existing*

That look is beyond explanation. I can't think of anything, anything in the world, that's like it; nothing that can capture it or express it or describe it. There are no words for that look.

That look, that was focused on me.

At her next meeting with the attorney, she is instructed to make a list of the things she has done to try and get better. She has kept her little black-leather, bible-paper daily planners for the last fourteen years, and now she sits down and patiently makes a note of each appointment. The result is staggering: 226 individual therapy sessions, 39 group therapy sessions, 21 family constellation days, 146 vocal yoga sessions, 118 physical therapy sessions, 58 classes in the Feldenkrais Method, 16 consultations with a nutritionist, and 37 sessions of osteopathy and other methods. She doesn't count the drama classes or the yoga and Pilates lessons, those thousands of hours spent trying to feel her own body, or the singing and trumpet classes taken as part of the effort to better control her breathing, or the countless tests and exercises and the books on personal development and the websites; all that time spent shedding light on her endless sadness.

I have spent a fortune in both time and money to make it to today. If I hadn't had places where I could take off the mask year after year, where I could allow myself to cry, to seek, to maintain hope even at the edge of the abyss; if I hadn't been *born with a silver spoon in my mouth*, I would, without a doubt, be long dead by now, or shut up, perhaps, in a false life, a life made of waxed paper.

She gathers up all her courage to ask various people to write witness statements about her journey, so that a *body of corroborating evidence* can be compiled in support of the reclassification of her complaint. She gets muddled up in timid explanations at first, red-faced, but the more she talks, the more she gains in confidence and clarity. A victory.

She meets with the midwife who was so wonderfully supportive during the last tumultuous phase of her pregnancy. The woman offers to help without hesitation, as does one of her directors, her osteopath, and, with heartrending sincerity, her husband.

She goes back to see the nutritionist who treated her in late adolescence. From a sheet of Bristol paper unearthed in her archive, the doctor reads out a diagnosis of *bulimic hyperphagia*. I would have liked for her to use those words back then, *bulimic hyperphagia*. They would have made me feel better. They would have been my first words. I would have continued with words, and maybe I wouldn't have had to suffer through ten more years of bingeing. I was so hungry for healing words.

She looks up her first physical therapy practitioner, who remembers her with emotion, recalls their work and that session, the violence of her remembering, the raw tension of her body on the treatment table, her terrible, astonished words: *he is inside me; he put his fingers in my vagina.*

She goes to see her parents late one morning, still in the same apartment they lived in back then. She doesn't feel comfortable asking her mother to write a witness statement, but the attorney has insisted: *Maybe she'll remember the visit to the pediatrician the next day.* She's doing it for peace of mind; she doesn't have any expectations.

Her old room has been turned into her mother's office, and

when they sit down at the desk she remembers herself that day, in a stupor, curled up on the flowered duvet, pretending to read *Nobody's Boy*.

Her mother begins to talk. Yes, she remembers the visit to the doctor; she remembers exactly when the pediatrician parted her thighs to examine the little vagina, that frozen moment when instead of the vertical line she knew so well from having washed it, swaddled it, cared for it; instead of that line there was a space between parentheses. She remembers the pediatrician's words: *This is quite abnormal.* Silently, her mother pulls open one of the desk drawers, takes out a clean sheet of paper, draws a large set of parentheses, takes a ruler, measures the space between the symbols. *It was like that. There was a space between one and one and a half centimeters long,* she murmurs. *That image has stayed with me, very strongly. Something wasn't right; something was wrong, very wrong—but there was nothing else; no wounds, no bruises.* She is quiet for a moment. *You know, for me, rape meant with a penis, with blows and screams. It did not even occur to me. When you told me it was his fingers, that image in my head finally made sense.* That image, that ridiculous image buried in the folds of her memory, has waited for me to come looking for it, so that it could finally emerge and give me tangible proof that I didn't make any of it up, that I'm not crazy. All these years spent hammering on doors, and all I needed were two parentheses on a blank sheet of paper.

After that we had lunch together at the small table in the dining room overlooking the Seine, and for the first time, I opened up to her about how I had isolated myself, hidden myself away, frightened of being discovered, being rejected. How I'd tried to do better; how I'd struggled with myself; how very alone I'd felt. How I had missed them. *But you seemed so happy; you were always smiling and cheerful. Everyone talked about how you were the epitome of* joie de vivre. Yes, I love it more than anything, joy; I need joy the way you need air, and I grab for it with both hands whenever it comes along. Maybe you have to be truly unhappy in order to know joy, maybe joy is the flip side of tears. She listened to me, this perceptive and loving woman, and I remembered suddenly that this woman was Mommy, my Mommy, lost and now, finally, found.

Later, she visits the office of the pediatrician who cared for her and her brothers and sisters. He is still practicing, still has the same ridiculous bowl haircut. He is attentive and very sorry. He remembers, too, and though he doesn't say it, he seems to blame the dark wanderings to which she was subjected for so long on his own lack of words, his misdiagnosis on that day, the day after it happened. He writes, *She presented no signs of physical violence (neither contusions nor bruises). However, on the vulva between the labia minora there was a vertical gap between 1 and 1.5 cm in height, which showed no bleeding but was completely abnormal in a child of that age, which might have suggested a rupture of the hymen. In retrospect this may have been the result of vaginal penetration by fingers, which could be construed as rape.*

Construed as rape. My mother and the doctor have both fallen prey to the myth of *true* rape, the one with screams, blows and wounds, the one in which a penis penetrates a vagina, the one committed against scantily dressed young women by sleazy strangers hiding in parking lots. I remember the friend, horrified to learn that I had been raped as a child, who was so relieved when I specified that it was with the fingers. *Oh, okay, so it wasn't really rape, then. That's not quite so bad, at least.*

Yet, by far the most frequently occurring rapes are those perpetrated against children, with no physical violence other than penetration. Whether the rape is vaginal, anal, or oral, and no matter what is used in the attack—penis, fingers, objects—almost every person who is the victim of sexual assault in childhood develops chronic PTSD. Having been subjected to sexual violence in childhood remains the determining factor in one's health even fifty years later, and can shorten life expectancy by up to twenty years. How is it possible that, even in our overinformed society, this information is so little known?

Because her psychotherapist has passed away, his partner attests to her eleven years of individual therapy and three years of group therapy.

How I would have loved to share with him the overwhelming joy of finally putting a clinical name to the jellyfish: *post-traumatic stress disorder.* How I would have loved to be able to tell him that our long years spent searching together weren't in vain; that they made it possible for me to hang on long enough, and to snatch out of midair the unbelievable chance to finally start my life again.

The psychotherapist who codirected the therapy group and the family constellation days, a detail-oriented and attentive woman who is also a sexologist, a woman she trusts deeply, hesitates to write a statement. She invokes her sacrosanct duty of professional confidentiality, and it's difficult to convince her, to protest that no one is asking her to do anything but relate the facts. She eventually agrees, but she doesn't mention the family constellations, and reduces eleven years of individual therapy to the vague *several years.* I didn't understand why then, and I still don't. She advises me to *focus on the attacker and the rape and then tell that energy to leave and fly away to the farthest corner of the universe,* but I've already done that, and it wasn't enough.

She reads her psychiatrist's statement over and over, a thousand times. *The symptoms my patient presents are all compatible with the acts of sexual violence she describes, and can all be classified as belonging to the specific and chronic PTSD shown by victims of sexual violence in childhood. These disordes represent a major handicap and a significant health risk, and require regular psychotherapeutic care.*

She has a diagnosis. She is suffering from something that is part of an illness, something that can be treated and cured. The jellyfish are pathognomonic symptoms; the jellyfish are medical proof of what he did to her.

I'm not crazy. I'm not worthless. I'm not weak. I'm not violent. It's just that, one day in May, a man snatched me up, and he annihilated me.

One morning in the psychiatrist's waiting room, there is a ghostly young woman sitting across from her. She recognizes the ghost; it was her yesterday evening, unable to sleep, sliding into the toy-filled water of a forgotten bath, sitting with her knees clasped to her chest, swaying gently, her heart icy. She would love to put her arms around this young woman and warm her up; stroke her long, dark hair; help her come back to herself. Looking at the girl's pale skin, her tensed features and hollow eyes, she realizes how far she, herself, has come. Despite the roller coaster, the frequent crashes, the blanks and flagellations, hope has risen to the top.

The psychiatrist advises her to go back to the place where he raped her, in her childhood stairwell. So, on one autumn day she goes back, not to see her parents, even to say a quick hello—no, on this day she is there to climb the stairs. A girlfriend comes with her; in order to avoid bumping into anyone, they go down through the Jardins du Trocadéro and along the path she always took when she was little, the one leading home from the playground. She doesn't speak much, her heart heavy. They enter the lobby of her building. *I don't remember which floor it was; let's just go up, it'll come to me.* She climbs, and suddenly, between two floors, she stops. *It was here.* The little white paper bag with the Carambars and the yellow plastic bottle were on the corner of this step. *He stopped there. I was a few steps above him, right here, and then*

his eyes
his hard eyes
his big adult hands my dress lifts
my panties drop
his hand takes mine and rubs it
soft floppy damp strange
his other hand between my thighs
his voice saying horrible things
you like it's good you're a nice girl
you want it don't you I can tell you like it
and
and

It all goes so blurry and confusing after his hard eyes.

When he'd finished, I went up the stairs. She climbs a few steps. She is struggling, as dazed now as she was then. She concentrates: right, the knee bending and the calf lifting and then lowering; left, the foot pressing on the step; right; left. A mechanical body following the feet—are they her feet? It keeps following, a body that is suddenly brittle and resistant, suddenly hostile. Another body entirely. And time stretches as she climbs; space distends, and she feels, she knows, that a few steps down, he has finished with her and her beautiful life.

She reaches the landing and stands, unmoving. *He's there, on the stairs, between floors, giving the "friend" speech, making me swear, making me promise.* She takes a deep breath, turns around, goes back down. Delicately, carefully. At the cursed step, she sits down, and she wraps her arms around herself, and she holds herself. Gently. For a long time.

The burning in her vagina stops. The big, dirty fingers are gone.

A few days later, in view of the evidence presented, in

particular the pediatrician's attestation, the examining magistrate approves the petition for reclassification, ordering *additional charges to be brought by the prosecution for acts of rape committed against Adélaïde Bon.*

Rape. Four letters, and in them, my ticket back to my homeland. We don't really know much about words at nine years old; at nine, we take words as they come. In the stairwell that day, words turned upside down, and after that I could only speak in opposites, and my native language became a foreign one. I've been talking nonsense all these years; I ran as fast as I could behind words that forked on my tongue; I ruined myself trying to find words of confidence, the words from before, the words from my childhood.

Words outline the horizon of our thoughts, so when words lie, when you replace *enemy* with *friend*, *violence* with *pleasure*, *rape* with *touching*, *pedocriminal* with plain *pedophile*, and *victim* with *guilty party*, the horizon is a line of barbed wire that keeps you from ever leaving the camp.

Having brought a civil suit, she now prepares to be the subject of an expert's psychological report. Her attorney advises her to be concrete, to give detailed explanations of her symptoms and their effects on her life, and not to forget that the expert's report will be read aloud to the whole court during the trial. Her psychiatrist counsels her to be on her guard, to remember that the things victims confide are all too often used against them, that it is very rare for an expert to be trained in the specificities of sexual violence and its consequences. Not to divulge anything about her private life that isn't connected to the rape. To remain evasive about symptoms that might be harshly judged. To make sure that, for once, she doesn't minimize anything.

When she makes an appointment with the expert on the phone, she asks if she should bring any specific papers, such as the medical attestations used in the reclassification of her suit. No, the expert says; she has her own copy of the entire file, naturally.

The office is furnished so luxuriously that she's intimidated, but the expert smiles at her and reads aloud the various questions she must answer. She asks about her family, what everyone does for a living, her childhood, her adolescence. She asks her if she has ever taken drugs. Defiantly: *Yes, I tried marijuana, but it only made the dark thoughts worse, so*

I stopped pretty quickly. What she doesn't say is that *pretty quickly* still lasted for years, or that she ingested plenty of other illicit substances as well. *Dark thoughts? What do you mean, exactly?* She explains by describing the first memory that occurs to her, the one from when she was in sixth grade and gave an interminable solo presentation on the Holocaust.

"Did any members of your family die in the Holocaust?"

"No."

"What impact did the war have on your family?"

"My grandfather was a hero of the Liberation, but my fascination with the death camps, that was something else; it was—"

The expert isn't listening, she decides. *This report is on his side.*

The expert asks her about her training, her profession.

"I'm an actress and a voice reader, and I lead theatre and writing workshops on gender equality."

"Ah, I see, gender theory! Look, I mean, believing that men and women are identical is really ridiculous; you can see it from earliest childhood; little boys like to roughhouse, and little girls play with dolls."

Adélaïde sighs, weary in advance. *There's no such thing as gender theory. There are only gender studies, which are extremely varied and often really interesting. Gender researchers analyze social constructions of the genders, not their nature.* In her workshops, she has seen all too often the human cost of sexist stereotypes and has plenty of experiences of her own to share on the subject, but the expert just keeps spouting clichés, so she takes a breath, gets a grip on herself. She mustn't disclose anything about her feminist engagement; experts often use that to negate victims' words. She waits.

Later: *You're a beautiful woman, still young. Your real problem is that you don't love yourself. Just love yourself a little more!*

"Loving yourself when you feel dirty isn't quite that simple."

"But you're letting him win by thinking that! You're the

one letting him win! You have to fight; learn to take make the most of life! Every day, try to focus on little moments of happiness—the Coué method—it works! You're too sensitive; too fragile. I mean, what is a rape, exactly? Fifteen minutes of your life? Fingers in your vagina? You know, there are so many other people out there suffering, people who have had truly terrible things happen to them. It's like with accidents and comas, you can either come out of them intact or have your whole life devastated; it just depends on your personality. Look at Marie Laforêt; she was raped, too!"

She bursts into tears. The expert keeps going, softly, in the pedantic tone some people use with small children. *I'm pushing you a bit, but it's only to help you. You shouldn't just let go. You say becoming an actress was only a default choice, but it's really good, being an actress! You think too much, and the theater sublimates that, which is excellent for you.* She focuses, gathers herself. Calms herself. She mustn't let her guard down. The expert repeats her comparison of rape with accidents, which she seems to find particularly apt, and the idea—as false as it is common—that there are some people who deal better than others with sexual violence because they've chosen to.

She recounts the facts. When she reaches the moment of her arrival in the apartment building: *Hadn't anyone ever told you that you shouldn't let strangers inside?*

"Uh . . . yes, of course. But he was very nice, and . . . I mean, I was nine years old. I didn't know there were such evil people in the world."

The expert nods, knowingly. *Your childhood was too sheltered.*

When she gets to the part with the murderous glint in the man's eyes, that precise moment when she dissociated from herself, sudden terror rips through her like a blizzard of nails. Her mouth opens soundlessly. Seeing her that way, white and frozen, the expert panics. *Oh no no, no, this isn't the place, no; this isn't the time; you have to pull yourself together, do you hear me? Let's move on to something else; tell me what happened after that.* She makes a titanic effort to come back to take in some air to relax her jaw; she manages to stand up, catch her breath, take a few steps. She apologizes. She sits back down. The expert quotes La Rochefoucauld—*Neither the sun nor death can be looked at steadily*—and theorizes, *You saw your own death; that's why you're so distressed. That's what is difficult for you, not the rape. You absolutely must work with your psychiatrist on your fear of death. He isn't a killer; he wouldn't have killed you; but that's what you believed.*

The expert asks her to list her own strengths and weaknesses, and then gives her two questionnaires full of convoluted, intrusive questions. Something is expected of her here, but she doesn't know what it is; she's being forced to play a game in which no one has told her the rules, a game in which she is the mouse.

Finally, she is asked to interpret any images she sees in a series of large ink-blots. Reaching the last one, as she is describing a pelvis that is dead but still giving birth: *Oh, thank goodness, that makes me feel better; all the other ones you told me were so terrible! I'm glad we're ending with something slightly positive.*

And then she is on her feet, pulling on her jacket. *So, the face-to-face meeting won't be a problem, right?* She freezes. *A face-to-face meeting with Giovanni Costa?* The other woman nods.

"Uh . . . yes, actually; yes, of course, that's a problem for me, I don't want to see him face-to-face."

"But you won't be alone, there will be attorneys there. Just like at the trial; no difference for you."

"No. No. Absolutely not. It isn't the same thing; it's a small group and we'll be right across from one another. No. I don't want him to look into my eyes. I'm afraid. I don't trust him."

The expert sighs.

In the corridor, as she walks her to the door: *The case will almost certainly be downgraded; it would be much better for you if it went before judges in a district court. The whole thing would be quicker and less painful.*

She, wrongly naïve, knows how often they declassify rape cases just to lighten the load on the circuit court. *I thought rape cases were only tried in circuit court?*

"Yes, that's right; it wouldn't be tried as a rape anymore, but it would still be much better for you."

"But it's important to me that what I went through be called what it was. Did you not read in the file that I had my initial complaint of sexual assault reclassified as a rape? Did you know the suspect is thought to have attacked and raped dozens of young girls at least? Do you not realize that they matched his DNA to four of them?"

The expert raises her eyebrows and huffs out a breath. *The circuit court's going to be very difficult for you. I wish you strength.* She dismisses her with an ice-cold handshake.

The next two weeks are a blur of insomnia, nightmares, binging and purging, and dark thoughts; two weeks of feeling worthless all over again; two weeks of blankness.

Later, when she tells her attorney about the appointment, the other woman is aghast. She has just received a copy of the expert's report and, for once, it seems accurate. In it, the expert concludes that *her reactions are characteristic of victims of sexual assault: fear for her life, peritraumatic dissociation and sexual blockage*; and that *she still displays extreme anxiety and very high levels of stress, as well as a fear of death.* What would the report have said if, as she usually does, she had minimized, trivialized, forced smiles and enthusiasm; if she had made jokes to avoid talking about it?

After the Christmas vacation, she meets with the examining magistrate for a a closed-door civil hearing to determine whether or not she will participate in the trial. The rapist's *modus operandi* was somewhat different with her; he talked to her about a bicycle rather than electrical circuits, and she is the only one who remembers masturbating him. The judge is hesitant: should the prosecution's case be weakened with slightly dissimilar testimony, or should this count be withdrawn?

She makes her way uncertainly through the maze of corridors in the Palais de Justice, with its officers on duty, its hurrying bailiffs, its distinguished attorneys and handcuffed defendants, and enters the judge's office: immense green plants and piles of file folders all over, on every table, all with the same five letters on their covers: COSTA.

She has to go over the details of the event. She is more precise this time, thanks to the memory work she is doing with her psychiatrist, but there are still so many questions she can't answer. Who lifted her dress? Who pulled down her underpants? Everything after the ice-cold look in his eyes is so blurry. Did he drop his trousers, or just take his penis out through his opened zipper? Why can't she remember his penis, when she vividly recalls the crocodile-skin belt with the gold buckle? And what happened then? When did he put his fingers in her vagina? What happened before she nodded her head over the railing of the stairs? How much time had passed?

The judge asks her what aftereffects the event has had on her life. She lists some of the jellyfish, but she doesn't have the words to describe what it really is, what it does to you, year after year, living inside-out. Not confiding anything in her parents, or her brother and sisters, or her friends. Cutting herself off from other people. Smiling. Concealing. Exhausting herself. Spending whole days outside herself. Living in exile, without anyone knowing about it.

T he public prosecutor's department releases its findings in the spring. Thirty-five victim files, including hers, have been selected for the indictment—hers because she told the examining magistrate about *the crocodile belt with the gold buckle*, a belt mentioned by other victims. All it took was that one detail.

Despite the colossal task undertaken by the two examining magistrates, thirty-seven additional complaints with similar *modi operandi* fall to the hatchet of the statute of limitations and are buried.

So, she will be in a circuit courtroom facing Giovanni Costa, who, she learns, is a seventy-something Italian with no fixed residence, a history of frequent imprisonment on house-breaking charges, and, perhaps, a serial rapist of little girls from affluent neighborhoods. All that's missing are the deep, dark woods, the seven-league boots, the still-sticky cutlass, and the glittering fairy passing through by chance, who has tapped me on the head with her magic wand.

I've been incredibly lucky. My parents listened to me when I was little, and took me to the police station to file a complaint. I had the emotional and financial resources to spend almost thirty years fighting. I was introduced to feminist thought and a network of supportive women. And finally, I was diagnosed and guided toward remembering by a wonderfully skilled and empathetic psychiatrist. In my whole happy childhood, I encountered violence only one time and, more than twenty years later, a man was arrested and put on trial for that violence. My complaint was neither dismissed nor declared to be lapsed. I had access to an attorney who was good-hearted and specifically trained in sexual violence, who supported me unhesitatingly in requesting the reclassification of my complaint and my bringing of a criminal suit. I was a little white girl from an upper-class neighborhood; I was always going to be believed, never prosecuted for defamation of character or judged for what I was wearing that day. Giovanni Costa is an immigrant offender; he has no family and isn't a person of note; he has no colleagues to protect him. He will surely be found guilty, and declared a monster in the eyes of the public.

But there aren't any ogres or fairies in ordinary life, and pedocriminals are often charming individuals. They are our relatives, our best friends, our neighbors, our teachers, our idols, members of the social elite. They are so convincing in their roles as respectable men, perfect mothers, dedicated professionals. In France, where nearly one child in five falls prey to sexual violence, it is rare for these young victims to be listened to and cared for, and even rarer for their attackers to be brought to justice. Our civilization has relied on the culture of rape, male domination, and the mistreatment of children for so many centuries. How many beaten children have there been among our ancestors; how many incestuously abused children; how many little girls married by force; how many women raped night after night under the filthy, secret pretense of marital duty? How many husbands, how many fathers have unquestioningly taken it as their right to blow off steam by administering a beating? The whole human race is the child of rape, a terrified child waiting for us on an ice floe.

S he sits in the park with her brother on a sunny Sunday afternoon. They watch their children playing, and her heart brims with words she has never been able to say. *Big brother, I was so unhappy, and I didn't understand why. I was furious—I was furious at all of you—I was furious at you, and I wanted to hurt you; I wanted to smash the frame of the beautiful family photo. I wanted to wipe the smiles off your faces. But now I understand; it took time, but I understand that it wasn't any of you; it was him, and now everything is possible again; maybe I can have a new life now, a complete life, a life I choose for myself. Big brother . . . even in all my projecting, all my nastiness, my anger, my absences, I have never, ever stopped loving you—all of you.* She writes these words on cocktail napkins, in notebooks, on the fly leaves of books, and she can see that the scattered notes are beginning to weave themselves into a rough outline, an outline that starts to make her think, make her dream: *a book?* She writes whenever she has a few minutes to spare; on public transportation, while the baby naps; on quiet evenings, she reads accounts of lives shattered to bits, articles, studies on sexual violence. She pushes herself, takes notes, marks up her readings with bright multicolored sticky notes. Gradually she swims further and further away from the shore and teaches herself, in the troughs of the waves, to distinguish between jellyfish and simple plastic bags. Sometimes the jellyfish become so stirred up that they swamp her entire body with semen and tears; when this happens, her productivity vanishes, and she knows she must not stay by herself, so she wanders the streets, and then, following Virginia Woolf's sound advice, she finally permits herself a room of her own, a desk in an office where some friends work. She finds that she can work well there, that it takes her only a few hours to write up workshop assessments that would have taken her two days before. She has no more time to lose; at thirty-four, she grants herself the time to write.

Encouraged by her psychiatrist, she publishes her first piece of writing on a website dedicated to the fight against sexual violence, but she doesn't dare sign her name to it. In the piece, she relates her experience of what psycho-traumatology professionals call *colonization*: loathsome images; perverse, violent thoughts that surge forcefully into the mind; monstrous impulses. She describes the blank hours, the desperate hours, the ones during which victims feel too much shame and guilt ever to talk about them.

After countless hesitations and U-turns, she reads the text aloud to her husband, and her trembling hand finds his, trusting.

A few days after the summer solstice, she arrives for her session with the psychiatrist, discouraged. Last night, the sneering horde of her old demons rose up in her heart without warning, bringing her to her knees, leaving her devastated and furious at their disgusting excretions. The psychiatrist listens to her, reminding her of the traumatic memory loss so common among raped children. *Maybe there was something inside you other than his fingers; maybe there are still some traumatic memories trapped in the little part of your brain called the amygdala?* She listens to the doctor, but she can't focus on the words; the pain in her jaw is too intense.

a musty smell filling her nostrils
invading her mouth her throat
thrown to her hands and knees on the carpet
gagging coughing puking
his dick
his dick on my lips his dick in my mouth
in my throat
his dick

He looked in my eyes, in which there was only my vulnerable childhood, and then he rammed his cock through my weak smile and down my throat. He asphyxiated me with his penis. The painful jaws, the coughing fits, the sudden choking sensation, the loathing of fellatio and the smell of cocks, the murderous anger when a man puts his hand on my head to force my mouth down on his penis, the sudden dread when I make myself vomit, the hideous images after my son's birth—all of it suddenly makes sense; every piece falls into place and I, too, find my place in this world that is straightening itself out, little by little, or maybe it's I, all of a sudden, who am standing up straight.

A few minutes of his big penis forcing its way inside my tiny mouth; a few minutes rediscovered, and with them, full possession of my past, the present finally logical and the future, possible. I'm finished going nowhere.

In the early summer, out in the countryside, seated in the shade on two little wooden stools in the warm, green-soaked air, my mother and I pick blackcurrants and redcurrants. I haven't planned it, have no idea I'm about to say it, when, in the middle of a boring everyday sentence I suddenly blurt out: *Mom, he also put his penis in my mouth*. I pronounce those words as if they don't have anything to do with me, as if I'm talking about something far in the past, a war in some distant country, and she receives them, and nods her head, and murmurs *My darling girl*, and our hands keep working, our fingers delicately plucking the red berries and the black berries; they don't stop, they keep going, and we talk about something else.

On a beautiful autumn evening, a few streets away from the restaurant where my husband and I are having dinner, people are killed.

In the newspapers, the dreary, humdrum past of the terrorists contrasts hideously with the rich, full, promising lives of each of the victims, living and dead. Nothing comes from hate except hate itself. I weep, I tremble, I scream, I read, and I hope. Might the subsequent deluge of articles on the post-traumatic stress disorder experienced by the survivors, and the appalling shortage of psycho-traumatologists in France, lead to some new careers; make some judges think twice; prompt some doctors to acquire more training?

And then, because any one of us could die tomorrow, and because life is short, I sit down at my desk. I reread my sky-blue notebooks, my dark-blue notebooks, my red notebooks, and my travel diaries. They are the rope I will use to descend into deep water, where the daily brain fogs are, the breath-holding, the lumps, the cracks and rifts, the throat that tightens and the desire that evaporates; where the innumerable army of tiny shadows will let me tell you, write to you, describe to you, you and the jellyfish; you, whose name and face I still don't know. But your smell—yes, I would know that anywhere, I could place it in a crowd. And even if my nose were blocked and I couldn't smell a thing, I would know, deep down, in the deepest part of me, deep in my very core, when you are there.

One morning, we are chatting in the office, the conversation jumping from topic to topic as we sip our coffees, and I bring up a subject close to my heart: the vital imprescriptibility of sexual crimes, mass crimes, unpunished crimes, crimes with delayed effects. In passing, I mention traumatic memory and traumatic amnesia. *Traumatic memory, how does that work?* And I, who love explaining things, who can't get enough of sharing my epiphanies with others, am off and running. Okay, so first, just remember three structures of the brain: the amygdala, the prefrontal cortex, and the hippocampus; pretty simple. I grab a marker and draw, on the sheet of paper, a small almond, *that's the amygdala*; a large oval, *there's the prefrontal cortex*; and a seahorse, *and that's the hippocampus*.

If something major happens to you, the amygdala sounds the alarm and allows you to react immediately. Imagine a car accident: BAM. The engine is on fire. Your amygdala tells the body to release adrenaline and all the other endogenous drugs you need to, let's say, get out of the car, run fifty meters away, and sit down.

By the time you're safe, the prefrontal cortex will have had time to analyze the situation, and the hippocampus will have compared it to its databank, and the two will then adjust, refine, or even shut down your response. I draw two lines connecting them to one another. *That's when you'll realize that your ribs hurt like hell and that the red you're seeing is blood trickling from your brow. You now have to think about lying down, pressing your hand to the cut, and taking out your phone with the other hand to call 911, and your hippocampus will even help you tell the firefighters exactly where you are. Then, day after day, this memory will be filed away in your autobiographical memory by the hippocampus and become one of those exciting, scary stories you tell at dinner parties.*

Now, on the other hand, if you're the victim of a rape, if you're in the presence of someone who has the intention of destroying you, annihilating you, reducing you to an object, the prefrontal cortex will try and try but it won't be able to analyze the situation. You're not an object, and this whole scene makes no sense. And the hippocampus will ransack its archives, but it won't find any response appropriate to the kind of hate it's dealing with. So, since it can't adjust or shut down the amygdala, the prefrontal cortex will at least keep you from dying of an overdose of adrenaline and other endogenous drugs. Overloading the amygdala can be life-threateningly risky for your body, so it has to trip the circuit in order to disconnect the amygdala. I erase the two connecting lines and isolate the amygdala with a thick black line.

The amygdala will keep sounding the alarm and recording everything that happens—your terror, your pain, his violence, his hatred, his perverseness—but your house is empty; your cortex is unemployed. It's as if you're a few steps away, an apathetic viewer, dissociated from yourself. The trauma continues, but you feel no more emotion; no more physical suffering; no more psychological suffering. The hippocampus is no longer receiving the necessary information either; it can't file this event away in your autobiographical memory, or locate the event in time and space. You won't consciously remember part of this day or even all if it; the memories that you do have will be confused, chaotic and disordered, as if they aren't real.

Your emotions and those of your attacker will be shut away together, so that, in your amygdala's traumatic memory there is a memory with no logic or point of reference; a raw, untreated emotional memory.

Later, when you're doing better, all it will take is a smell, a noise, a word, one of the thousand buried fragments of that scene, one of the thousand detonators, for that memory to explode and flood you with thoughts of hate and terror. You won't understand where these images are coming from, the violence, the horrible acts you inflict on yourself. You'll try to stop the suffering; you won't want to feel anything at all. You'll find unhealthy escape in bulimia, anorexia, compulsive masturbation, violent sexuality, pornography, drugs, self-harm, risk-taking tendencies, and so on—all sorts of dissociative behavior. It's a way of increasing your stress level in order to secrete enough endogenous hard drugs to numb yourself.

Or, rather than destroying yourself, you'll choose to destroy others. You'll prefer the impressive efficiency of hate as a means of dissociating. So you'll become the torturer; you'll anesthetize yourself by perpetuating horrors on others similar to the ones you lived through, betraying the victimized child you were just a little more each time, making yourself drunk on power, on acts of hate and lies, all to avoid confronting your own despair.

Aggressors are cowards. I don't understand our fascination with criminals. Rather than writing novels and TV series and shock-value tabloid shows about the careers of criminals, rather than turning them into monsters so we feel better about our own humanity, we should be erecting statues, writing biographies and screenplays, throwing parades, singing songs, and organizing festivals and bank holidays to celebrate the courage of the hundreds of millions of victims whose stories have never been listened to, but who manage to make it through the day alive, abandoned, beaten down, and so terribly alone.

The trial will begin in early spring. Still one more season to wait, sitting on the bare corner of a step; one last season, one last winter.

Session by session, solidly anchored to my psychiatrist, I move toward an unexpected word: healing. But I still bring moments of greyness and shadow with me to the office; my shadows are beacons, the sign of a buried memory, another memory to be exhumed, defused.

On my conviction that I am always the one chosen through spite, by default:

"The other little girl in your building, the one he spoke to you about; was she all right?"

"We barely knew each other; she wasn't very chatty, but I remember that her mom seemed kind of strange, and I found her dad intimidating."

"Her father might have been violent. Your attacker had chosen this girl carefully. It's quicker, less dangerous, even less strenuous to attack a person who has already been subjected to violence. A victim that hasn't been cared for dissociates almost instantaneously; aggressors know how to spot them; they know they won't struggle, and afterward they won't be able to say anything about it. The fact that you were a happy, healthy girl living in a close, loving family where spousal and domestic abuse played no role meant that it took more effort for him to dissociate you from yourself. That's undoubtedly why he went so far with you. To guarantee his own impunity."

"So, afterward, then, I was easier to prey on than other people? That's why I attract every pervert within a ten-mile radius?"

"Yes. Unfortunately, the principal risk factor for being subjected to violence is already having experienced it. But you are healing."

On the blinding pain in my jaws whenever I eat for pleasure:
his voice, muffled that way,
vibrating through his dirty penis in my mouth
You like that, don't you? You're a gourmand.

My revulsion whenever a lover touches my anus.
his fingers pressing
his big adult fingers spreading my buttocks apart
my rigid body
his fingers hurting his fingers forcing
his fingers
in me

Not a single orifice that you didn't soil. The words *rape of a minor* weren't enough for you; you wanted to be sure I'd never talk about it. You called in the full firing squad: *by vaginal, oral, and anal penetration.*

Session by session, the walls shift, and I discover what a huge thing it is to love when you are less mistrustful of yourself. Yes, I still feel I have to be watchful, and every time I hug my little boy or change his diaper or give him a bath, I methodically scrutinize each one of my thoughts, but nothing dirty comes now to disturb the clear water; the sickening images don't sully my laughter, my kisses, my cuddles.

As soon as I can, I write. Often, yoked to my desk, I'm working away and then, suddenly, the floor opens up, I falter and curl up in my chair. When the roaring fades, still stunned by the upsurge of the wave, I gently massage the soft skin of my left wrist, reddened and damp with saliva, marked with small, regular rectangles left by my teeth. No one has heard me scream; my terror is discreet, but now, even as the swell reaches full strength, my eyes are wide open and in the sea foam I can see shapes emerging. A few enormous, majestic jellyfish come toward me, extending their silky tentacles so I can braid them. Then I am Medusa, the granddaughter of the Earth and the Ocean, raped by Poseidon in the secrecy of a temple. I am innocence defiled, judged guilty and condemned to see my long hair transformed into snakes; they say I am the one whose gaze turns anyone who crosses my path to stone. I am the wild woman forced to hide in a cold, damp cave, I am the one whose head is cut off while she is sleeping, the one whose mutilated corpse strikes terror into the hearts of advancing armies. I am what remains of a woman after she has been raped. And writing it renews me, puts me back together, repairs me.

Two months before the trial date, I am reluctant to return to my attorney's office, where we will go over the *Order for the purposes of reclassification, partial dismissal, and indictment.* I end up having to drag myself there by the scruff of the neck.

First there is a summary of the inquiry and investigation and then, for each victim, the known facts. After two, three, four, five similar, terrible stories, I can't read anymore; my vision blurs and I'm dizzy, so I focus on the names of streets from my childhood. The street my primary school was on, rue de la Pompe; my high school, rue de la Tour; my pediatrician, boulevard Émile-Augier; the stadium, boulevard Lannes; my girlfriends' houses, rue Raynouard, avenue Victor-Hugo, boulevard Flandrin, rue Eugène-Manuel; the streets I took often, and certainly every school day: rue Scheffer; rue Chernovitz, rue Louis-David, rue Lekain, rue Vineuse, and avenue Raymond-Poincaré; the ones near my mother's office: rue Saint-Simon; rue du Bac; and the ones where I sometimes played, square Lamartine and parc Monceau.

You had your habits; you knew the building's hallways, the service staircases, the floors that were quiet and undisturbed. Year after year, you haunted the same streets in the same neighborhoods. Many of the victims remembered seeing you several days in a row, months later. One of them saw you two years afterward, in the inner courtyard of her building; you saw her, and waved at her. You were so sure of yourself. A few attentive mothers even called the police every time they found their daughters paralyzed with terror at having encountered you again, but the officers always arrived too late.

One year after you raped me, I was coming back home via rue Scheffer, and on the opposite sidewalk a man called out to me. His wife was pregnant, and he needed help carrying some heavy bags up the service stairs. Heart frozen, body robotic, I didn't answer, didn't turn my head, didn't look at the man. I concentrated, left, right; I kept walking, left, right; I acted like I hadn't heard; I wanted no part of those words, they hadn't been meant for me, left, right; there was some mistake. That man was you, Giovanni, wasn't it?

The trial is in three weeks, and my inflatable face is once again showing the signs of binge-eating. I've gained fifteen pounds in the last few months.

One evening I go to see a play in which a friend is performing. I get to the theater early and drink a glass of red wine in the crowded lobby. A few steps away from me is an actress I knew at ESAD twenty years ago; she is radiant, elegantly dressed in a wide, dark-blue scarf and beautiful brown ankle-boots. I hide behind a post. I stink of death that night; I don't have the strength to pretend, to smile, to come up with answers to *How are you?* and *What are you up to these days? Are you still acting?*

I wish I no longer panicked at the sight of a familiar and friendly face, dropping my gaze and pretending I haven't noticed. No one knows how much effort it takes for me to talk, how I just cannot do it some days. I still feel so unworthy of them all. All those years ruled by shame, avoidance, mistrust. I missed so many opportunities, derailed so many meetings, stifled so many desires, that if I planted a little white cross each time, my life would look like a vast military cemetery.

The play starts. I'm sitting in the first row. The actors are wonderful, and suddenly a woman shoots up and dances, her body blazing, and my heart is so heavy, my face wet with tears. I curl in on myself, in my seat.

At the end of the play I am so happy for the beautiful

theatrical adventure that has opened up for my friend and, as it often does, joy carries me toward other people. I have the courage to greet the woman I saw in the lobby; she exclaims, sincerely, *Adélaïde, you're still so beautiful!* What a chasm there is between us. I live so little in the face she sees. I blush, and thank her, and try to accept the compliment.

On a day in May, my eyes that had seen almost nothing stared, powerless, at the face of a man as it twisted, distorted, emptied itself of all its humanity. On that day I took Ugliness, Contempt, and Evil into the very depths of my soul. More Evil than I could ever comprehend. That lasted for a long time, didn't it, Giovanni? Your face is still there, hidden inside me; I see it every day underneath my own tired features, my cellulite and my flabby belly.

In a few weeks, you will be there. I hope seeing you again will drive out your face as it looked on that day, expel it from my body. I hope I will finally be able to hand your features back to you, and stop getting them mixed up with my own.

The trial starts in two weeks and is supposed to last eight days. I don't know if my dad or my brother and sisters know about it. I've mentioned it two or three times to my mother; I'm always the one who brings it up, and even then, I don't say much. They don't know what happened in our stairwell that day. They've heard me say I had my complaint reclassified as *rape*, and that I've filed a civil suit, and they know I'm trying to write a book about it.

My friends offer to come and support me, but the ones I want most to have by my side are my mom and dad, my brother and sisters. I've been lucky enough that a man has been arrested, that there are other victims to corroborate my account, that my mother remembers it, and that the law believes me, and I want to grab on to that luck and use it as a megaphone to say to my parents and siblings, *Look at me; for years I have carried hatred and terror, violence and ugliness. Look at me; they weren't mine; they belonged to him, the one sitting in the dock. There are the years you and I have spent not knowing each other anymore except through my excessive behaviors and our silences. Look at me; I'm right here in front of you now, stripped bare, my body bruised and ruined. Look at me. I need to able, finally, to break down in your arms. I need you all to come and stand by my side.*

I take the opportunity of an e-mail exchange to give them the trial dates and suggest that they join me at the Palais de

Justice at lunchtime. Only one of my sisters replies, the one who understands the depth of the impact in light of her own experiences. She has set aside three full days to come and support me.

A few days later, my courage boosted by a few glasses of wine, I talk to one of my cousins about it at a party. He listens to me, and is supportive and encouraging. I want to weave crowns of laurel leaves for him and my sister, and parade them through the city in a flower-bedecked chariot in triumph and jubilation.

The next Sunday at a family lunch, I gather up my courage and focus on a single goal: to say to them, *It's going to be hard, and I need you.* I don't want to regret not having asked.

Sitting at the big table, I wait for someone to give me an opening, to respond to my lunch invitation, to ask for details about this trial we've never talked about, to express concern. They chat about everyone's upcoming vacation plans; who's going where; the American election; the kids. The meal is passing and I can't find the right time to speak up; I smile in all directions and pass the plates and cut the tarts. Suddenly there is a pause in the conversation, and I think to myself, *now*, but even that tiny hesitation is too long, and someone has already started talking about something else, and the children are running in and out, and then it's time for coffee in the living room, and all the smaller subsidiary conversations, and then everyone is standing up and getting ready to leave. I have tears in my eyes. I bite my tongue, look frantically around for my sweater. My sister-in-law, standing at the door: *What's new with your trial?* I manage to choke out *It's going to be hard* and run into the dining room to cry; then I wipe my eyes and pinch my cheeks and go back into the foyer with a wide smile. We say goodbye in our turn and take the elevator down. The minute we're outside, I burst into tears.

I needed love and comfort so desperately. I blame myself for not knowing how to ask for it; I blame them for not seeing it, or daring to give it anyway.

A few days later, my mother calls me. She will be there, and my dad too. They will take turns being with me, and she suggests calling my brother and sisters and organizing shifts.

The waves grow calm inside me, and in the blue clearness I can see the ocean floor.

I was worried by my father's silence. I write to him: *Mom told me you're going to try to come. I can't imagine how difficult it must be for a father to talk about this kind of thing with his daughter, but it would mean a lot for me if you were there. I need you. I'm going to need my Dad's arms around me.* Simple words, and yet it has taken me years to be able to say them.

Exceeding my expectations, they'll all come. My husband, my mom and dad, my sisters, my brother, my aunts, a cousin. Every day, the curtain separating us will draw back a bit further. I will let them take me in their arms, and in our tentative embraces, so many things will be expressed without the words needing to be said.

My friends will be there too, the ones who feel able, the ones who won't falter when they see me fall apart.

They will all be there, standing together by my side.

III

D ay one of the trial. I took care with my appearance, carefully choosing a flattering, discreet, comfortable outfit; I waxed and moisturized my legs last night, and washed my hair. I have a date with myself.

Outside, the sky is heavy with the promise of showers to come. I ride my bike between puddles left after last night's rain, my eyes stinging, my heart braced and ready. The streets are empty. In front of a high school, a cleverly arranged pyramid of green garbage bins announces an upcoming protest against a new labor law. I have barely arrived in Île de la Cité when the sky opens and rain pours down. I chain my bike to a guardrail and run for shelter in the café, where I find my mother and her worried smile already waiting. I draw deep breaths, let them out in quick splutters, study the faces of the young women at the counter. *Which ones are the other victims?* We gulp down our coffee and cross the boulevard du Palais, pass through the metal detector, up the vast stone staircase, into the grey solemnity of the immense lobby. Then we climb staircase K, past the guards on duty, and into the Victor Hugo courtroom.

The room is paneled in dark wood, its grey-blue ceiling covered in stucco relief figures, its walls dotted with alcoves. To the right, these alcoves frame wide windows overlooking the main stone staircase, the high metal gates, and the boulevard du Palais. To the left, one of them contains the dock, a dead end enclosed by wood and tinted glass. Giovanni Costa will enter that box any minute now, and from that vantage point he will be facing the benches allocated to the plaintiffs. He will only be able to see our profiles, unless we choose to turn toward him. Next to the dock is the court clerk, whose desk forms one end of the large semicircle where the jurors will sit, with the presiding magistrate at their center, flanked on either side by his two assessors. At the other end of the semicircle are the prosecuting attorney's desk and the small table occupied by the court bailiff. Then, on either side of the central aisle there are heavy, polished wooden benches, defense on the left, prosecution on the right. To the rear of those is a long balustrade, behind which are three narrow rows of chairs. In the center of the room is the witness stand, a small wood and copper box, its handrail polished by all the hands that have clung to it, like a lifeline. There, you swear to speak without hate, without fear; to tell the truth and nothing but the truth. There, words are weighty. They determine the course of entire lives.

The room rustles with murmured conversations and coats draped across laps. *There are a lot of us,* I tell myself. *Many are on our side.*

Giovanni Costa enters the dock. I look closely at his face and I don't recognize him; I can't see anything of the May man in this disheveled old man with his nylon tracksuit top and shabby T-shirt, his bald head fringed with grey hair and sunken eyes. I don't recognize him, this paunchy old man who sits down rather stiffly, but I stare at him anyway, I can't tear my eyes away, and suddenly his eyes flare up and, from his platform, he studies the people in the room, one by one. My stomach hurts. Panic grips me. *He's looking for us.* I'm struggling to breathe. His eyes are sweeping closer. I grip the hand of my psychiatrist, who is sitting next to me. *He's going to see me.* I can't bring myself to turn my head, and then suddenly I feel the blow. His hard eyes bore into mine, my muscles tense as my body is suffused with hatred. I can't catch my breath. The man from the stairwell, the May man, the man from twenty-six years ago and every day since then, is him: Giovanni Costa.

When the judge enters, the whole room stands and then sits again silently, and, as he reads out a list of twenty-four names, the jurors for this court session, the realization gradually washes over me that the people in the gallery aren't victims and their loved ones; no, they're just average Joes who are going to be selected at random to decide our fate.

Several recusals later the room is almost empty. Six jurors have taken their places near the judge. A good-looking, thirtyish man with a carefully trimmed beard. A man with a plump, kind face. A tired-looking old man. An elegant woman with beautifully coiffed hair. Another man who's the spitting image of Charles Berling. A bright-eyed woman wearing glasses.

Four alternate jurors. A dignified, well-dressed young man. A little old lady with white hair held back by a wide black band. A dynamic young retired woman. A woman with a round face framed by brown hair.

The judge is inscrutable with his long red robe and impassive expression. He speaks deliberately, his words affable and well thought-out.

The prosecuting attorney is a huge man with a short salt-and-pepper beard and tortoiseshell glasses.

Since the lawyer who represented Giovanni Costa during the preliminary inquiry has retired, two young Secrétaires de la Conférence, public defenders, have been chosen to represent him. Their skills in oratory earned them this assignment exactly two weeks ago, and while the one thousand seven hundred and ninety-four pages of documents in the Costa case fit on a USB stick, they can hardly have had enough time to get the full measure of their client. The judge has barely finished reading out their names when Costa stands up and dismisses them. The judge objects that, though the defendant has the right to impose silence on his attorneys, he cannot represent himself at a civil trial. Costa makes a questionable joke about *beautiful women*. I have a hard time understanding him; he speaks with a thick Italian accent.

As their names are called, several victims cited as witnesses stand up and leave the room. When a person isn't there to reply to their name being called, the judge says, *Set aside*, looking more and more perplexed as the list of absences grows longer. As the long procession of protestors passes in the street outside the sounds of their whistles and snatches of their slogans drift in through the windows. There are two of us sitting silently on the plaintiffs' bench: an angular young woman with a sweet expression, and me.

Giovanni Costa reigns.

The judge begins to read out to the court the list of charges, and at the second one—*Having, in Paris, on 13 May 1990, on French soil and within a time period not covered by the statute of limitations on public prosecution, by means of violence, coercion, threat, or surprise committed an act of sexual penetration on the person of Adélaïde Bon, in this case notably by introducing a finger into the vagina of the victim, with the circumstance that these acts were committed against a minor of less than fifteen years of age, being born on 1 March 1981*—Costa leaps up and, pressing his hands against the tinted window, shouts:

"You're the one who's a child-rapist, collabo!"

I'm in the stairwell of my building
terrified
paralyzed
I can't breathe

"Mr. Costa, you'll have your chance to speak later."

"You cocksucker, child-rapist, it's all lies; I'm not a rapist!"

"Mr. Costa."

"You're talking bullshit; go fuck yourself!"

"Mr. Costa."

"There's no one here! Where are the victims! Where are the plaintiffs? Fuck off!"

"Mr. Costa, I'm telling you to calm down."

"Where are the witnesses, you cocksucker?"

"Mr. Costa, if you don't calm down I'm going to have to have you removed from the courtroom for the rest of the day."

"Where are they, asshole? Bastard! You fucking slave of Italy! Where are they?"

He is taken out of the dock by two officers. My body collapses.

In the renewed quiet, the judge continues reading the list of martyrs. I don't hear any of it over my own sobbing.

Now that the judge has named the crime, the defendant has shown a little of the violence he is capable of, and the victim has burst into ancient tears, everything is in its place.

After the lunch recess, a police officer from the Juvenile Protection Brigade takes the stand. It's the captain who called me on that winter night three years ago, and with whom I met a few months later.

Proceedings in circuit court take place verbally. The presiding judge is the only member of the jury panel familiar with the case, so the police captain takes the jurors and assessors through the long-term investigation that led to *the electrician*'s arrest. He has the muted voice of a person who doesn't like public speaking, and everyone leans forward to hear him better.

Twenty charges of rape, attempted rape, and sexual assault of minors between 1983 and 1984.

Twenty charges of rape, attempted rape, and sexual assault of minors between 1990 and 1991.

Thirty charges of rape, attempted rape, and sexual assault of minors between 1994 and 2003.

Almost all of them committed in west Paris, by a balding man with a singsong voice; a mature man who asked little girls for help. He often mentioned a light bulb, an electrical box, or an electricity meter. He manipulated their soft little hearts, isolated them, pretended he was giving them a leg up and shoved his paws between their thighs, took off their clothes, groped their breasts, rubbed his genitals against their vulvas and buttocks. He slapped them if they cried. He penetrated them with his fingers and his penis. Sometimes he ejaculated on their clothes.

Four little girls were taken to the Forensic Emergency Medical Service, and their semen-stained garments placed under seal.

An initial investigation was conducted from 1990 to 1993 and ended in dismissal; the perpetrator was never identified.

From 1996 to 1998, the Juvenile Protection Brigade established a report of fifty-six similar events involving someone nicknamed *the electrician*. A second investigation ended in dismissal; the perpetrator was never identified.

In 2001 a suspect was taken in for questioning. The police forensic department retrieved from the clothing placed under seal (three pairs of small white underpants, a pair of jogging suit bottoms, and a grey t-shirt) traces of DNA from a single individual. The DNA did not match the suspect questioned.

A third investigation was conducted from 2002 to 2005 and ended in dismissal, with the perpetrator remaining unidentified. The reports were filed away. End of story.

But then a woman came along, slender and determined; she had been an investigator with the crime squad for a long time, and had decided to devote part of her retirement to the reopening of cold cases. It was she who unearthed *the electrician*'s file from the archives. After much painstaking work and hundreds of telephone calls, she managed to locate the various items of evidence under seal and, thanks to recent scientific advances, she was able to obtain a more precise genotype from the public prosecutor's office in 2010.

It is thanks to this heroine working behind the scenes, whose name I don't even know, and thanks to the successive teams who preserved the sealed evidence that, in early 2011, *the electrician*'s DNA was entered into the French National DNA Database, a project near and dear to the father of Sigrid, my friend from high school.

In April 2012, after an altercation between neighbors, one Giovanni Costa was taken into custody. His arrest record reveals a past loaded with convictions for theft, so a diligent police officer takes a sample of his DNA to enter it into the Database. In May, it is revealed that this DNA is a match with *the electrician*'s.

A third investigation began in June and the case was reopened. Investigators tracked down the original records, located and re-interviewed numerous victims, and arrested Giovanni Costa.

He was detained in October while sitting at a bus stop at Richelieu-Drouot, not far from the shops receiving stolen goods with which he often worked; sitting in the same place it had been his habit to sit in for years, where those who knew him always knew where to find him. He wasn't a hunted man.

Once arrested, Giovanni Costa denied the facts, refused to acknowledge the evidence of DNA, claimed to be the victim of a plot hatched between a female Italian police officer and a group of black market operators; accused everyone around him (especially the women) of slander; insisted that he had a doppelgänger, that he'd never had any trouble seducing French whores, that he was an Italian stallion at whom women were constantly throwing themselves.

In more than twenty years with the Child Protection Brigade, I have never come across an individual like this.

The female police inspector who takes the witness stand next recalls questioning Costa: *We spread photos of the little girls out on the table, and he became enraged. "I am not a rapist! Odds are the sperm on their underpants is from their father or grandfather; ask them!" He threw the photos on the floor and screamed at me, "Bitch, I bet you let all the dogs fuck you," before ripping out the cables of the computer that was recording the session.*

None of the reported assaults happened during any of periods during which he was incarcerated for burglary.

When he speaks of his *profession*, burglary, he describes a *modus operandi* that corresponds to his young victims' recollections on every point. *I passed myself off as an electrical or gas repairman. I'd wait quietly in the lobby of the building for someone to come in, so that I could access the service staircase. Once I was in there I would say I was there to fix something. I'd show them where the meter was; I'd give them a boost if there was no stepladder, and I'd tell them to watch and make sure it was working correctly. During that time, I'd go into the bedroom and take whatever I could, usually jewelry, and then leave.*

The genetic profile taken from the four items of clothing matches his own, and it is a profile that emerges in the general population less than one time every seven billion.

Then the detective adds, her voice resonating in the silent room, *In the ten years I have worked with the Juvenile Protection Brigade, I've seen plenty of sexual predators, but none have left an impression on me the way he did, both because of the sheer number of his victims and due to his lack of consideration for them, or for anyone. I can say from my own experience that you don't become a sexual pedocriminal at fifty. Violence allows him to avoid any questions.*

What has Giovanni Costa's life been for his seventy-eight years? No one knows, or at least they don't know much.

He was born in 1938 in Villa Rosa, a small town in Sicily, into a devout Catholic household. *No one in the family has seen him since he left home in 1958*, his sister-in-law has told the Italian police. He called her once in 1989, broke, to ask her to pay his attorney's fees during his umpteenth incarceration. After that she transferred small sums from the inheritance left him by his father, in monthly installments—despite the last wishes of his father, who had died two years earlier stipulating that his son wouldn't get any money if it didn't make it back for his funeral. When the inheritance ran out, Giovanni never called again.

His police record gives only a sketchy outline of his comings and goings:

Between the ages of twenty-one and twenty-nine he was in Belgium, already a habitual housebreaker and frequently in police custody. He was imprisoned six times in Charleroi, Liège, and Brussels for attempted theft, theft, fencing stolen goods, assault and battery, impersonation fraud, forgery, and falsification of records.

By age thirty-one he was in France, imprisoned in Marseille for theft and weapons possession, and then in Saint-Ouen for theft, receiving and possessing stolen goods, and weapons possession. He spent six months in prison, got out for a few months, and then was arrested again for attempted theft in Paris and then Colombes. After his umpteenth offense he was ordered to be deported and refused future entry at La Queue-en-Brie; at this point he started using different false identities, including that of Salvatore Trapani, a school friend who had emigrated to the United States.

At forty-one he was arrested in Paris for attempted theft with housebreaking and spent a year in prison. Two Parisian convictions later there were two more years in prison for theft with housebreaking, receiving stolen goods, forgery of an official document, and infringement of a deportation order. He had barely been released when he was back in again at age forty-nine, convicted in Paris and sentenced to four years in prison for theft, et cetera. He was released on parole two years later.

He received another four-year prison term at age fifty-four for similar offenses, but was paroled again in less than two years.

At sixty-six he was convicted in Paris of theft with housebreaking, illegal weapons possession, forgery, and falsification of records.

At seventy-four he was convicted in Paris of intentional violence with a weapon and concealment of evidence. It was then, while he was in custody, that an eager officer took a sample of his DNA.

How repetitive life is for people who are bent on destroying it.

The investigating officer called to the witness stand to testify about Costa's character and history confines herself to summarizing what he told her during their interviews in prison; she has not been able to verify any of his rambling flights of fancy. He has never held a paid job. He claims to have worked off the books in restoration and cabinetmaking; to have studied law in Switzerland in 1957, to have lived in London between 1972 and 1974. He claims to steal only from the rich. He has spent most of his time living in hotels. He has balls. He claims to have stayed with the same woman for fourteen years, but he can't remember her first name. He is passionately fond of horse racing, prostitutes, and shoes, especially crocodile-skin ones, boasting that he has bought dozens of pairs when things were good. He has always been careful to have perfectly pedicured feet (he had just done them when he was arrested). He claims that the rapist is his double, but he can provide no alibis, can't remember where he was on any of the dates of the incidents because he travels so much. Oh, wait, yes, for one of the four victims whose underpants were smeared with his DNA, *It's all lies*; he spent that day watching the final Italy-Brazil World Cup football match at the Hotel Worringer in Dusseldorf (a match that didn't take place until the following month). He is a thief, not a rapist; he is educated, Italian, desirable, virile, a stallion, a real man.

I think he wanted me to put him in touch with the examining magistrate, the officer concludes.

The young woman sitting with me on the plaintiffs' bench is called to the stand. An image of her face back then is projected onto the screens in the courtroom. It's a birthday photo, taken a few months before the rape. Behind the candles and the chocolate cake decorated with Smarties, a little girl winks at us, her smile gap-toothed and her bangs rumpled. And here she is, years later, standing very straight, her hands grasping the rail tightly. Simply, in a firm voice with no hint of a tremor, she relates the events of the dark day, and her subsequent survival. When she joins me back on the bench we clasp hands, briefly, tightly.

Next, the judge reads the deposition given by a young woman who has not attended the trial; it's one of the two girls whose names I recognized from the Victim Notification, the one with whom I went to high school. The judge reads her account of savagery, and I think of that plump, timid girl who seemed so nice, whom I ran into so often and knew so little. I hope there was someone to hold her hand.

Since reading depositions is quicker than listening to the halting testimony of victims on the witness stand, after the twenty-fourth *Set aside* of the morning, the foresighted judge removes a full day of arguments.

In the evening, as I prepare myself to testify the next day, my stomach in knots, men and women from every part of French society hold their first Nuit Debout protest at the catafalque that the place de la République has become, attack by attack. The protestors restoree to the statues covered in sodden notes and extinguished candles the luster of their allegorical significance: Liberté, Égalité, Solidarité.

Day two. A new young woman, her body so rigid I'm afraid it might break, sits trembling on the same bench as me. Giovanni Costa watches us, and she has barely taken two steps toward the witness stand to give evidence when he starts champing at the bit; the moment she opens her mouth speak he hurls insults at the judge, calling him a *motherfucker*, etc. Once again, he is summarily bundled out of the courtroom for the rest of the day.

I am called to testify. I move forward, shaky and disappointed. I would have liked for him to be seated in the dock while I stood at the bar; I would have liked for him to hear what I have to say, for it to be my turn to speak and his to be silent. I would have liked to describe for him in detail each one of my wounds. I would have liked for the judge to suggest, once I was finished, that he account for them.

This afternoon, as is my right as plaintiff, I have asked that my psychiatrist, Doctor Salmona, be called as an expert witness.

Radiating passion and authority, with the simplicity often displayed by those with great souls, she explains, in precise clinical terms and quoting studies, what it means to live a whole life after being raped.

When she has finished her summary, the jurors, the judge, and the prosecuting attorney are all allowed to ask questions.

"I apologize for the technical question, but does the hymen have to be broken for it to be considered rape?"

"Absolutely not. The hymen is a permeable membrane. In two-thirds of the rapes committed against children, no tears are noted in the hymen."

"Is it really possible to forget that you've been raped?"

"Yes, sometimes for decades. The majority of children who have been subjected to sexual violence present complete or fragmentary traumatic amnesia related to the disconnection mechanism triggered by the brain to protect itself from the extreme stress generated by this violence."

"Can the memories a person does have of the rape be made up, or altered?"

"Absolutely not. These are not conscious autobiographical memories which are located in time and become dulled as the years pass, and which can be intentionally recalled, described, analyzed, or transformed. A traumatic memory generated by rape is located outside time. It inflicts itself as if it's happening again right now; it repeats without being altered at all, with the same emotional weight it had the first time, the same details. The years have no effect on it. It's like the black box in an airplane. It is involuntary, invasive, and uncontrollable, and its recurrences are indistinguishable from one another."

"Is it possible to recover from a rape?"

"Yes, fortunately, if the victim receives specific treatment. She will have to relive the traumatic events in order to integrate them finally into her autobiographical memory, but to do that she must be guided and cared for by someone trained in post-traumatic disorders."

"Is sexual attraction to children something that actually exists?"

"No. Pedocriminal behavior has nothing to do with desire or sexuality. Violence generates extreme stress in the aggressor, an overload of the amygdala, triggering the same psycho-traumatic mechanisms as in his victim—except that he is using the victim as an analgesic; he chooses to provoke this emotional storm in order to obtain a very high production of endogenous hard drugs, and then disconnection and emotional anesthesia. He wants to keep himself from suffering; he wants to feel invincible and all-powerful, and, crime after crime, he develops a more and more severe addiction to extreme violence. The purer the victim, the more abhorrent the crime, the stronger the anesthetic effect will be. Pedocriminals are violence junkies."

There are no legal records for the years since 2003. Where were you, Giovanni? What did you do to your victims so none of them would file a complaint?

Clara, Marguerite, Adélaïde, Stéphanie, Leïla, Myriam, Sophia, Alice, Melinda, Maria, Sophie, Marie, Anna, Mathilda, Clotilde, Sybille, Juliette, Philippine, Julia. In the end, nineteen of us are there to testify.

Fourteen plaintiffs, nine of whom will have filed their cases a few days or hours or even minutes before taking the stand, all describing the days of horror preceding their appearance here, all trembling with the determination and resolve they have had to muster to testify at this trial.

One of the very first victims to have brought a civil suit has failed to appear, as has her attorney. The bailiff and the clerk call her and leave messages, but she doesn't call back. They contact the attorney. *She no longer wishes to testify, or to be represented; she is terrified.* Thirteen young women will follow her example, disobeying the summons to appear and choosing to be found in contempt of court rather than break the seals on that hideous day and its long aftermath.

At lunch in the place du Châtelet with my parents and sister on the third day of the trial, I recognize one of those thirteen women. I recognize her because she also happens to be the daughter of famous parents, and I did a Google search for her face one solitary evening. She waits for someone for a long time, standing outside the restaurant, and I want to go up to her and say *Excuse me; we don't know each other but we were victims of the same man. His trial is happening just a few steps away from here. I just wanted to tell you, to warn you. But is that maybe why you're here; why you came back to France?* I cling to that stupid idea for a moment, and then I chicken out. She is radiant right now; she seems so serene, and I'm afraid of the black, oily film my words will smear on the brightness of the day.

The morning after, when the judge reads her deposition in her absence, and makes clear the despair of this young woman who was only six years old when Costa raped her; the extent of the catastrophe; everything she has had to do to survive; I am angry at myself for not having dared to reach out.

And then there are all the women for whom the time limit has expired, whose testimony has not been asked for by the court.

I've written all the first names of the absent women on the flyleaf of my notebook, and every day of the trial I bring them there with me. Céline, Anaïs, Caroline, Constance, Anne, Sophie, Toinon, Charlotte, Aurore, Alice, Anne, Juliette, Gwendoline, Sophie, Sandra, Marine, Louise, Joëlle, Élisabeth, Ludivine, Julie, Marine, Laura, Anaïs, Florence, Elsa, Perrine, Albane, Chloé, Victoria, Ingrid, Alicia, Raphaëlle, Véronique, Laure, Élise, Delphine, Vanessa, Saïda, Céline, Yun, Marie-Eugénie, Sandra, Claire, Amélie, Patricia, Sophie, Marie-Christine, Stéphanie, Tatiana, Adeline, Élodie, Marine.

And there are the women—all the women—for whom the crimes were never reported.

And there is you, Giovanni, who have dedicated your whole life to stealing and raping.

W *here are the witnesses? I want to go face to face with the witnesses! All you have to do is put those girls who are accusing me right here in front of me! Let them face me! They have to come here and tell me in person that I raped them! Let me confront them! Bring me the victims who are accusing me! Put one woman right here face-to-face with me to say that I raped her. Just one! I want to see her face-to-face!* you demanded repeatedly, every time you were questioned—so vehement were you, in fact, that the judge refused to send you a full copy of the court documents, on the grounds that *there are risks of stress for the plaintiffs if Mr. Costa were obtain copies of their hearings or their contact information.*

But by the evening of the fourth day, all the testimonies of the victims included in the court order have been heard, and yet you weren't there. You haven't answered a single question, or been cross-examined even briefly, or confronted any of us.

On the first two days, your behavior got you expelled from the courtroom at the very start of the session; you called the presiding judge a *motherfucker* five or six times, and after that you let yourself be transferred from the remand center to the holding cells in the Palais de Justice; then you refused to leave your cell, hurling insults at the bailiff sent to inform you of your obligation to be present in the morning, and at the clerk responsible for informing you about the day's proceedings in the evening.

Every morning you make us wait in vain for more than an hour. Every evening you force the judge to implore a bailiff to come to the Palais the next morning. The trial can't start until you have reiterated, in the bailiff's presence, your refusal to appear—and there are only two people in Paris willing to take on such a poorly paid job.

I imagine you letting your hatred macerate in the stinking urine in your damp basement cell, but it doesn't make me feel better. How can I get rid of you without seeing you?

An attorney reads aloud to the empty dock a letter written by one victim's mother. *We have been brave enough to come and testify. Will you be honest enough to respond to us?* Your absence is your answer. You give us nothing. Nothing to analyze, nothing to debate, nothing to confront. You're above the law. This trial has nothing to do with you. We don't exist. For you, we have never existed.

After the first witness statement, the disappointed journalists have deserted the press section. Without the housebreaking rapist of little rich girls, without the snarling outbursts of the monster, the story lacks spice. Hate is sexier than pain. Some Somali pirates are on trial not far away; that's more of an attention-grabber than the awful banality of raped little girls.

So, in the face of the jeering disdain of the empty dock and the inquisitive faces of the jurors, our hands gripping the bar as if it were a life raft, we have one by one taken off our pretty, carefully constructed masks; we have lowered our shields; we have let flow tears too long unshed, and we have tried to capture devastation in words.

Every testimony, one after the other, fits me as if I were giving it myself. And in the outstretched mirrors of their stories I rid myself, little by little, of yours.

"I met this man when I was ten, and—" long silence.
"I'd rather answer questions." She bursts into tears.

*After lunch at home, I was going back to school with my lit-
tle sister when kind of an old man called out to me that he
needed help changing a light bulb in a stairwell.*

*I had stayed home from school with a cold that day, and
someone rang the doorbell. I looked out the peephole, but I did-
n't see anyone, so I thought the concierge must have left the mail
on the doormat. I opened the door and there was a man on the
stairs. He came back up when he saw me, and said he was the
building's electrician, and asked if I was home alone.*

*I'd had an argument with my parents and I was riding my
bike fast so I'd get home first. The chain came off my bike and
this man came up out of nowhere and said he'd fix it if I helped
him change a light bulb.*

*I was crossing the Parc Monceau, which was packed because
it was lunchtime. I was going with my brother to play football
and a gardener told us he'd pay us ten francs to help him move
some flowerpots.*

*An old man told me he was having trouble walking and took
my arm.*

*His wife was pregnant and he had some heavy things to carry.
He was an old man, so I held the door open for him.*

*A man told me that his wife was pregnant and their plumb-
ing had stopped working.*

He was very embarrassed to have to ask me.

*I always tried to be helpful to people. And he said he'd give
me some ice cream.*

*I was scared to tell afterward, but he'd promised me ten
francs.*

*I grew up in a Catholic family; I was a Girl Scout. I was
taught always to be useful.*

He wasn't scary; I felt kind of sorry for him.
I was brought up to help people if they needed it.
I wanted to help him fix the meter.
I knew I wasn't supposed to talk to strangers, but he seemed
so nice, and so embarrassed to be asking me for help.
I was an obedient little girl.

> *he glanced at the caretaker's office several times*
> *suddenly I was really scared*
> *he asked my little brother to stay there*
> *and keep an eye on something*
> *he told my friend to wait downstairs*
> *he took me up the service staircase*
> *he took me down behind the dumpsters*
> *he took me into the cellar*

> *"Follow me or I'll strangle you," I was really afraid,*
> *I followed him*

> *there was a grey box on the wall*
> *I could see that it wasn't working*
> *there was a sort of skylight up above*
> *there was a handle that needed to be turned*
> *the light was working but I didn't dare say anything*

> *I remember*—long silence—*the look in his eyes*

> *I was afraid he'd kill me so I did what he told me to*
> *I was paralyzed with terror*
> *I thought he was going to kill me*

> *I have the expression in his eyes*—she breaks off

> *he tried to lift me up a few times my feet*

never left the ground but every time my T-shirt
rode up a little more he acted like he was trying
to carry me he squeezed my breasts harder and harder
he lifted me up several times as he was doing it
he had his hands on my chest and then
—uh—what happened?

he grabbed my bottom as he was lifting me
he asked me how much I weighed
and then he grabbed my buttocks

"You're very pretty," he licked my neck
"Let's kiss, okay? I'm not going to eat you"
he kissed me on the lips
"Be nice to me," he kissed me
hard everywhere on my neck and face
he told me that I was pretty and that I was nice
he licked my cheek
"I'm not going to eat your tits; I'm married,"
he licked my breasts
he kissed me three times
and then he put his whole hand in my mouth

I managed to get away I ran down the stairs
he was snickering loudly I yelled at my little sister
to run to open the door
it was winter I was wearing several layers he had to give up on
undressing me completely I had on overalls that
tied around the neck he spent time
fumbling with the knot and got angry because he couldn't undo it

my pants bothered him he pulled them down slowly he said
he was allergic to jeans so I had to take off my shorts
even though they weren't made of denim

he had some kind of metal tool in his hand
I was afraid he would
hit me with it so I obeyed and took off my underpants

I was totally naked all of a sudden, I don't know how

I was facing him; he asked me to hold him by the neck
he held me pressed against him he made gestures to
show me that if I resisted he would strangle me
he pressed me against the wall and rubbed himself
against my buttocks it was very hard
inside his pants "You're crying for no reason; you're
just a kid. The other ones didn't cry like that," he
opened his zipper he made me look at his willy he slapped me
"I don't like kids who cry," he set me down on the desk I didn't
have my trousers on anymore he was
fiddling around with my vagina I was really afraid I cried a lot
he hit me with his fist he put two fingers in
my vagina it hurt a lot and I wanted to scream but I
couldn't make a sound he started laughing he put his fingers
inside he smelled them he licked them he had kind of a
muffled laugh it scalded me I asked him to stop he slapped
me four or five times he laughed he made fun of
my fear he wiggled his fingers around in my vagina: "You'll feel
better after this," it hurt really badly he started doing it again,
"I'm only going to put my fingers in,
stop crying," then he licked his
hand and I was crying he touched just inside my anus with his
fingers with his penis, "Stop crying or I'll give you
spanking," he couldn't get his penis inside me
with me pressed against the wall so he made me lie down on the
stairs he spread my legs it hurt so much
"Shut up, people will think I'm trying to rape you."

I remember certain details exactly and at the same
time it's very confused in my head I don't remember
very much at all I think I've suppressed a lot of stuff
I think there are a lot of things that have disappeared from
my memory they found sperm in my underpants I
didn't remember anything I don't remember but if I
said it at the time it's definitely true I wasn't the kind
of little girl who would lie I said I'd seen his penis but
now I'm not sure I can't remember—she cries—
it's just a blank space to me

afterward he told me he was a decent man
that he was married with kids
that he had two children a boy and a girl that he
called himself "Salvator the savior."

"You've been a good girl for me," he took me to the
bakery to buy me the treat he'd promised me I was
paralyzed I didn't dare say anything to the baker who
knew me very well he gave me four or five ten-franc coins
he told me I'd done him a big favor that
I'd earned a reward he put a coin in my hand
he wanted to give me some money ten francs twenty francs
thirty francs I refused he made me swear not to tell,
"We're friends now."

he wanted us to see each other again
he asked me what I was doing on
Wednesday he asked me what time I finished school
he wanted to see me again he suggested that we make
a date for later he made me promise to come back

he went away he left the door open I was terrorized I
didn't dare leave the room I was afraid he'd come back

he stayed nearby all afternoon
he waited for me for hours outside the front door of the building

my mom found me limp and catatonic
it was a neighbor on our floor who called the police
when the officers asked me to show them what he'd
touched in the apartment, uh, he only touched me
there were no fingerprints anywhere
he made me open all the doors for him all the drawers
move the stool handle the meter

there were so many police officers at the station I was terrified
I didn't say much
I knew I'd done something wrong that I'd gone with a stranger
I didn't tell everything
I felt guilty for having held the door for him
I didn't tell everything
I was ashamed I didn't talk about the touching I just
wanted the interview to be over
I didn't dare tell about the erect penis and plus I didn't
know the words to describe it

my dad was beside himself he went and searched for him all
over the neighborhood
all night he moved the family
to the South the next year
it was the mother of one of my friends who
told the police officers about me
my parents were told
but they never spoke to me about it
my father was very angry at me he said I
hadn't acted correctly because I hadn't screamed
my mother was so shocked that we suddenly
moved away from Paris the next year

the move had disastrous consequences for the whole family
my parents told me it was a secret
we never talked about it again
my father told me not to tell anyone because people
would look at me differently
I grew up a recluse until my twenty-first birthday my parents
never let me leave the house alone again no
more birthday parties no more school outings
no more sleepovers with my friends no more school trips away
nothing
except maybe a burger at McDonalds with my mother
I couldn't talk to anyone about it
even the psychotherapist
my parents took me to see
at home we never spoke about it it was taboo
I had to keep it all inside me I
became locked inside myself I based my whole
identity on suspicion

I felt so guilty

I told my best friend and she made fun of me
in front of everyone
they all knew about it at school someone left a message on
our voice mail at home "You shouldn't have reported it
to the police. We're going to get you, whore"
some girls in my class wrote me a threatening letter making
me believe it came from him

did it have an impact on my life?
she shrugs her shoulders and can't manage
to get out another word.
the aftereffects?—long silence—
I was lucky—her voice breaks.

it was an immense trauma
it was a sort of breaking it isolated me completely
it caused me a lot of problems afterward
—she dissolves into tears.
he completely destroyed me—silence.
it held me back in everything
it ruined my life

it's being completely alone in the forest at night
it's a very physical feeling
that comes out of nowhere at any time
for a long time before I fell asleep I could see
images of what had happened to me
I started sucking my thumb again
I had a lot of nightmares
even now I'm still scared of the dark
I couldn't go for a walk alone—she breaks into tears—
in my neighborhood for months I didn't dare
go back to high school I saw him
everywhere my performance at school fell apart
I couldn't concentrate at all
I've had trouble concentrating ever since
it dominates everything I buried myself
in studying I became anorexic
I became bulimic

I was afraid of all men even my father
I didn't want my dad to hug me anymore
it destroyed my relationship with my father he never
understood the impact it had had on me

my first sexual experience?—her voice breaks,
she can't say anything else.

*I still remember his fingers inside me I am terrified
at the moment of penetration I can still feel his
fingers pushing between the lips of my vagina I only
have intercourse with my husband out of a sense of obligation I
don't get any pleasure out of it*

*I've developed a system of invisibility
no one sees me
I became bulimic
so men wouldn't see me
I became suspicious of everyone
it's better not to be too nice in life
I have a lot of trouble trusting
especially men I tend to freeze up
and I can't say no I'm always afraid
of losing control around men
I'm very suspicious I can't bear to be alone
in close quarters with a man who has
authority over me so passing my driver's test
going to the doctor
being in my boss's office is impossible for me*

*I've been so emotionally fragile since it happened to me
sometimes I faint
I live in constant fear
I think about it all the time it's like a kind of cloud
that's always in my head
I feel abnormal, broken
I've had a feeling of anxiety inside me since then
that infects so much else
I was depressed for a long time
I'm afraid all the time
I've withdrawn into myself I'm always very nervous
I have chronic migraines*

I have so many fears and anxieties that I don't understand
I've been in psychotherapy for years

I freeze up whenever anyone tries to touch me
I can't even get a massage
I'm afraid whenever anyone comes near me if someone
comes too close or touches me I want to hit them

I've always been extremely scared of men and yet I've
often fallen for macho men violent men who treated
women like shit
my relationships with men have always been difficult
complicated painful a while ago I fell
in love with a woman I'm happy with her
and it makes me sick to say it to say that this beautiful
relationship is partly due to him but I do think
there's a link to what he did to me

I had forgotten everything but at a party when I was eighteen a
guy pressed me against a wall to kiss me everything
came rushing back I collapsed to the floor

when the police called me three years ago I burst into
tears it took me right back to that horrible place
all of the memories rose up when the police contacted me
it had all been buried inside me everything came back
when the police inspector called me
between the call from the Juvenile Brigade and the time
I went down to file a new complaint we'd been trying
to have a baby but I stopped ovulating I started having
panic attacks again it was like I was functioning in slow motion

the more I think about it the more traumatic it is
even though it happened so long ago

*

when I was pregnant I was so afraid
of contaminating my baby
during both of my pregnancies everything started up again I
had serious
neurological and cardiac problems
I bathe my children compulsively I panic very easily
especially since my children were born

my husband isn't aware
so testifying today is complicated
I don't want him to know
I haven't been able to tell my parents he was arrested
or that there was going to be a trial
I've never told my husband,
I made up an excuse to come here today
this is the first time I've ever spoken about it
in front of people

when I recognized him in the courtroom
it was such a shock I couldn't move
on the first day of the trial I didn't recognize him from the back
but as soon as he turned around
my stomach was tied in knots
it's the man I saw on the first day
—her whole body tenses
it's him—barely audible

I'm a psychologist.
I do combat sports; I became a boxer.
I'm an emergency pediatric surgeon.
I'm a law student; I'd like to be a judge, maybe in juvenile court.
I came because it might help keep other people from going
through this.

I decided to come today to conquer this feeling of shame and guilt.

I would like to bring that day to a close.

The day after you trapped us, we all woke up in our pretty children's bedrooms and we kept going to school, smiling at the nice lady, saying *thank you*. We got by; we were lucky; we were alive; it could have been worse. We didn't talk about it anymore, or we didn't say much. We each built a life for ourselves. We tried our best to pile both difficult and pleasant experiences on top of that day; we left it in the cellar and forgot it; we put up partitions and hallways and opened windows, built a frame with our own hands, and though we sensed, in some confused way, that the building had a defect, we didn't know what it was. So we learned to paper over the cracks, the panic attacks; to tuck our anxiety away in the attics. We invited guests over and felt, finally, as if we were living in homes of our own.

But after the phone call from the Juvenile Protection Brigade, little black dots appeared on our walls. We pressed on them with our fingertips, and the walls crumbled. We looked at our doors and they had become tunnels and underpasses; we pricked up our ears and the walls, the floor, the ceiling began to screech and grate; the acrid smell of saliva and feces suddenly hit us. We ran down the stairs and every step vanished in a puff of dark smoke. We'd barely made it outside when this beautiful house that cost us so much collapsed in a heap of rubble. All at once.

Young women, nervous and naked, demanding that justice be served.

Marguerite, aged nine, tells the police, *He put his pee-pee in my privates and in my bottom; he hurt me with his pee-pee. I started crying and he put me back down. Then he started again but it still hurt.* Marguerite's underwear was found to be stained with sperm; the doctor from the forensic medical unit confirmed that she had been vaginally and anally penetrated. Marguerite, when re-interviewed three years ago, was extremely reluctant to relive that day she had tried so desperately to forget, and limited herself to saying as little as possible. During the investigation, Marguerite's complaint of rape was downgraded to sexual assault.

Philippine told the captain three years ago that *He put his finger into my vagina; I could feel that there was something going in and out.* No one told Philippine that it was rape, or that she could request a reclassification. The legal time limit on Philippine's complaint of sexual assault has lapsed, and her request to bring a civil suit is rejected.

Mathilda, to the captain, three years ago: *I could feel him pushing his fingers between the lips of my vagina.* On the witness stand, Mathilda testifies that she remembers his fingers inside her; I wish her attorney had jumped up and pointed out to the jurors that that was rape—but, for lack of reclassification, Giovanni Costa is charged only with sexual assault.

Juliette was one of the first victims to bring a civil suit. She breaks off suddenly on the witness stand; she loses track of what she was saying, can't remember. The initial charge of sexual assault has expired, and when her attorney requests a reclassification as attempted rape, Juliette is subjected to a dreadful salvo from the judge: *Inadmissible findings, definitive referral order, dismissal of charges, termination of prosecution in your case!* This impassive judge, seemingly unruffled by Costa's insults, flushes red with anger just this once. Juliette has annoyed him by describing a whole life of pain with a face that

is maddeningly calm, her air detached and her voice mono-
tone. The bailiff asks me to comfort her during the recess that
follows, and her inertia exasperates me, too; I want to shake
her. I've forgotten that this seeming indifference should be a
warning sign; that the more a person is dissociated from herself, the more anesthetized she is emotionally, the worse the
violence she has been exposed to, and the more danger she is
in of being exposed to it again. That afternoon I took her
blankness for a lack of intelligence. I judged her harshly. I
didn't recognize her.

Julia's claim of sexual assault has expired. She came to testify anyway, and stayed. Julia breaks down in tears when she
describes the months that followed the attack, when she was
terrified by the idea of walking anywhere alone. She has never
stopped being terrified.

Legal terms cannot possibly describe the hatred. Testimony
after testimony, twenty years later, no matter what he did to
them, every one of them is in pieces.

And I, who have resolved not to mention either the forced
fellatio or the anal digital penetration; to describe neither his
moist penis in my tiny mouth nor his big fingers in my anus,
to keep to the deposition I gave three years ago so that my
testimony won't lose any credibility—I force myself to keep
silent about the fact that I know, now, that there were other
things that happened.

And there is Laura. The prosecuting attorney introduces
into the debate her 2003 deposition concerning rape against a
minor committed in 1983, its time limit expired, but imputed
to Giovanni Costa. It took twenty years for this woman to find
the strength to go into a police station and file a complaint.

How many, like her, weren't listened to by their families? How many of them have carried you with them all these years, completely alone, Giovanni?

It's four days into the trial and I have started to love the starched formality of the circuit court; the long red robes, the ermine, the long black robes, the officers, the polished language and rarefied phrasing. I love the high-backed, dark wooden benches that allow me to hide my face from the court when I'm overwhelmed. I love the scale, the fasces, the eye, the axe, the hand of Justice—all those interlaced stucco symbols that dominate the courtroom. I love the discreet support of the moved, silent police officers, and the clumsy gentleness with which they treat us. I love the sudden, obvious sisterhood that has sprung up between the victims, and the intelligence and humanity of the prosecuting attorney who never stops specifying, pointing out, informing. I love the improvised picnics we have in the big marble hallway, watched over by a bronze statue of Justice, her right hand lifted, tablets of the law pressed to her heart. I love the various friends who arrive each day to take turns supporting me. I love it when my sister suddenly comes over to hug me tightly; I love it that this trial is also, a little bit, a trial for that smooth talker who scarred her life. I love watching my aunt asking, in the public section, who is the mother of whom; listening with one ear to my father conversing about Géorgie with the defense lawyer; knowing that my mother is cupping her ear frantically to hear the prosecuting attorney. And on this sunny afternoon, when my aunt is taking advantage of a recess to take us to visit Saint-Chapelle, I love the soothing peace of the blue stained glass windows in the heart of chaos. I love my husband's shaky, precise notes, his sweet messages, his hugs. I love watching the jurors' faces lose their arrogance, testimony after testimony; I love how, as the days pass, the dark circles under their eyes deepen and their masks slip off. I love these jurors, who sometimes venture to look at us, to give us some little sign, just long enough for a flutter of the eyelids; to show us their empathy, their humanity.

Through loving, through crying, I gradually claim ownership of the space-time of Justice. Here, where my whole existence is contained in a few words, where I am forever nine years old, where order is brought to the chaos of the world, where horror is named—here, I finally feel as if I am in a safe place, where I don't have to pretend. I can reassemble myself. I can, finally, resemble myself.

On this morning of the fifth day it is the psychologists' turn to talk. The ones who have written expert's reports on four of the plaintiffs, and the ones who have written experts reports on the accused.

I dread the testimony of the first one. She is the one who tossed me out a year and a half ago. She has compiled reports on three of us.

She links the first subject's *psychological fragility, neurotic profile, and poor sense of identity* to something completely unrelated to the rape—a serious accident, or a death in the family. She presents only a *very mild* case of post-traumatic stress disorder. Yet, this young woman in tears on the witness stand described the profound catatonia into which Giovanni Costa had plunged her; she remembered almost nothing, had no idea why there was semen found in her underwear, didn't remember having seen his genitals—but later, at age nine, she began seeing the image of an erect penis superimposed on every man she encountered. She went through two periods of intense depression. While still a young girl she was again the victim of serious sexual violence; first a gang sexual assault and then another rape. She has told us that she is on the alert every second of her life, and that as the trial approached her sexuality once again withered to nothingness.

The second subject is me, and though the psychologist irritates me by talking in detail about my family and my studies, all is forgiven with her next words: *Severe post-traumatic stress disorder compatible with the events described.* Why such a different diagnosis? Because I had been prepared for that meeting with the expert. I'd had help establishing links and understanding which damages he was solely responsible for inflicting. I'd been trained not to minimize anything anymore, not to make apologies for myself the way I'd done in the past.

The third subject is Sybille, twenty-one years old and a stunning beauty. Sybille, in tears, her powerful body curled on the plaintiffs' bench, trembling so much that even today my hands remember it. Sybille, who said, *He completely destroyed me; I live in constant fear.* Yet the expert has not diagnosed Sybille with PTSD, because *in her, repression syndrome supplants repetition syndrome.* What does that mean? She doesn't bother to explain it to the jury.

At the end of her report, out of all the men and women who have taken their turn on the witness stand she is the only one to receive a sympathetic aside from the judge: *I know how your profession is under a great deal of pressure at the moment.* She answers, swatting away invisible flies with the back of her hand, *We're on the side of Ethics.*

The second expert keeps us waiting for three hours and he is as silver-tongued as full of praise: never has he seen *such a successful psychological recovery;* his subject, *with her considerable intellectual powers,* has suffered *no post-traumatic repercussions* and is *fully restored to health;* the aftereffects on her life *are almost nonexistent today.* Her attorney comes back at him. *Oh, is that right? And yet she hasn't stopped crying since the trial began; she clings to her therapy sessions like a life preserver!* And then it is the expert's turn to flounder, to justify himself. *Well, the preparation of the expert's report involves subjecting the person to a reactivation, a mini-trauma, and we pay close attention to the way in which she reacts. I stand by my diagnosis.* The prosecuting attorney persists, citing traumatic memory and traumatic amnesia, and the expert entangles himself further and further in muddled explanations.

How ugly is ignorance concealed beneath a veneer of learned airs.

How shameful that, in France, doctors, psychologists, police officers, and judges are not systematically trained in the specific symptoms connected to sexual violence.

Especially considering that, when a victim of sexual violence is correctly identified, diagnosed, and cared for, she heals.

It is now time for the testimony of the experts who examined Giovanni Costa. We're desperate to hear what they're going to say, after spending the last five days with nothing but the vacant chair in the empty dock and the thousand grotesque characters that have been projected into that seat: Costa the Italian, the stallion, the man with balls; Costa the racegoer, the heavy gambler, the pedicure enthusiast with the crocodile shoes; Costa the gentleman housebreaker, the itinerant international miscreant; Costa the poor old man wrongly accused, the victim of a conspiracy; Costa the solitary, the marginalized; Costa the infuriated man spitting insults, the old pervert, the lecher offering sweets at the school exits; Costa the ogre, the devourer of tender little girls; Costa the sick, the unhinged, the antisocial. Who is Costa?

None of them is familiar to me; none of them resembles the man who set up housekeeping inside me so long ago. No, the man I know, I have seen his features in the testimonies of the other girls; I have seen it in his jeering laughter, his slaps, and his inside-out words.

The first psychologist is away on vacation and has told the clerk firmly that she refuses to make the journey back. The judge reads her report; in it she concludes that he has a *paranoid personality structure*. Oh, really? I know full well that he's much too intelligent to believe his own bedtime stories.

The girl that went to the same high school as I did hasn't come to the trial, but I run into her shortly afterward. She's a psychologist. She's not angry at Costa; *The poor man is a sociopath, antisocial, he's sick.* She's especially incensed at the police for not questioning him before the trial. I bristle. I can't believe she's saying this; I don't buy it. It doesn't shed light on anything for me. It doesn't correspond to what I know about him in the deepest part of my soul. He doesn't act impulsively. He doesn't jump out and grab us; he waits. Patiently, for days on end. He chooses the child, the place, the setting. He approaches us under false pretenses; he nicely tells us lies: *My wife is pregnant; I have two children, nine and ten years old; I'm looking for a room for my older boy; I really need help.* He lays his trap methodically; he instills terror drop by drop and then he uses us sexually, and the more he degrades us, the more he jeers at us, the greater his triumph. When we're dissociated, confused, at his mercy, he speaks poisonous words to us, words with false bottoms. *You like that/perverted; I can see that you like it/pig; this will make you pretty/bitch, this will do you good/whore; it feels good, hmm, you love it/depraved; doesn't that feel better, hmm/slut; you were made for this/dirty; you're a gourmand/slag.* And last come the padlock words: *It's our secret, I'm your friend, it's between you and me, don't tell anyone, they won't understand, promise me you'll never say anything, you're a nice girl, here, to thank you for helping me, I'll give you ten-twenty-thirty francs, some sweets, an ice cream.*

Now a second expert takes the stand. And his words ring true; his words make amends. *The accused bears full and complete responsibility for the acts in question. There are no psychiatric grounds for the alteration or abrogation of his criminal responsibility.*

He displays paranoid delusions of persecution, but because it is unusual for someone presenting this type of personality disorder to commit rapes, this may be another manipulation tactic.

It is probable that we are dealing with an extreme and perverse manipulator, a conclusion supported by the exceptional number of victims. I would remind the court that in France there is what we call the "dark figure" of victims of sexual violence; it is estimated that ninety percent of rape victims do not report the crime, and this figure is even larger for children. In this case you have made a list of seventy-two young victims. You can add a zero to that number.

In the frozen silence that follows, the judge calls a recess before the plaintiffs' pleading.

My attorney comes toward me, holding to her chest seven pages of twelve-point font; seven secret and painful pages, a condensed version of the worst moments of my existence. She has asked me to choose, from my sky-blue notebooks, some passages that would give the jurors a palpable sense of the suffering I'd endured over the years. Before entering them into the debate in writing, she wants to read a few lines aloud. *Oh, no! It's out of the question. My mom and my aunt and sister are here. I don't want them to hear that; it wasn't meant for them.*

But there is Marguerite; there is Sybille, there is Leïla, there are all these amazing, courageous girls who have taken the witness stand one after the other, there is our suffering, dismissed by amateur experts, so *yes*, so *all right*. I run out into the marble corridor to see my mother, and my sister and my aunt. *I'm sorry, my lawyer is going to read my private journals; I didn't want you to hear that; those words aren't for you, I'm sorry. I love you.*

My attorney starts to read. I hide my face on my wooden bench. I am ashamed that everyone is hearing my uglinesses laid bare.

When the reading is finished I stare fixedly at my hands, motionless, determined not to meet anyone's eyes. My aunt, my darling aunt, comes up behind me and presses her forehead against my trembling shoulders and wraps her arms tightly around me. *We really are useless; we had no idea.*

The judge reads out the questions to which he and the jurors will have to respond. Eighty-four principal questions, and twenty-three secondary ones. He has ensured that, for each victim, if Giovanni Costa is judged not guilty of rape or sexual assault, depending on the case, he can still be judged guilty of attempted rape or attempted sexual assault.

The closing arguments by the attorneys of the fourteen plaintiffs begin. In the parade of long black robes, each lawyer speaks in such a different style that it seems like a master class in pleading techniques.

The bellower, pointing his finger at the empty dock: *I'm asking you to crush the accused!*

The crafter of pretty phrases, the media favorite.

The skilled and vibrant: *There are two obstacles facing the child: the first one is that she must be listened to by her parents, and the second is that her parents must press charges. The women appearing here today are also here on behalf of the ones who are absent; of all those little girls encountered in the course of an entire life dedicated to inflicting pain.*

The indifferent one, who has spent the trial sending text messages, the one who had better things to do.

The awestruck and emotional: *My client, who is married and the mother of two children, told me she has never had sexual relations that weren't simply something to be endured.*

The technical one, the connoisseur of the articles of the law.

And the volcanic one, whose powerful thunderbolt of a speech will bring the day to a stunning close.

When I arrive at court on the morning of the sixth day, the officers on duty warn me: Costa is there. The presiding judge gathers together the attorneys for the plaintiffs who have not yet pled and warns them that the first one to speak will be copiously insulted; that they mustn't let themselves be thrown off by it. He leaves it to them to decide which of them will go first.

My husband sits next to me, his back very straight. I need all our love to contain my fear.

He enters the dock. He doesn't look at us. He aims a polite little smile at the judge and jurors and sits down. Every eye is fixed on him; when will he start shouting? One attorney approaches him, addresses him, scrutinizes him, glares at him, corners him, charges him, and yet nothing. He doesn't respond. He stays calm. He stays calm, but he is there; he can hear it all; and the words transform, they begin to build something, to ease the pain, to put things right. It's enough that he's finally here, sitting in the dock, with us sitting on the victims' bench, so the words can find their target, so that justice can be done.

Another attorney is speaking but I can't hear it; you're looking at me, Giovanni, sneering at me, and my whole being is focused on holding your gaze, on not dissociating this time, on breathing, on feeling my anger scald me the whole time your piercing eyes try to force mine to look away. Finally, you're the one who turns, and in that tiny victory lies the threshold of my new life.

The final attorney for the plaintiffs, charismatic, militant and well-known, concludes his speech. *These little girls may have coated themselves with a layer of concrete and then a layer of lead on top of that, but it is rotten inside. It poisoned their whole life.*

Giovanni Costa comes back after the lunch break. I have to pinch myself to believe it's real.

The prosecuting attorney rises, immense. He is no longer leaning over the small microphone; he stands over the accused, towering him, nailing Costa's eyes with his own, and begins his closing speech. *Mr. Costa, you have been either absent or odious and outrageous, but you are going to have to answer for all these acts.* He wears a flowing red ermine-trimmed robe; his voice is clear and resonant. *Mr. Costa, nineteen of your victims have come here to testify. You weren't there; you didn't deign to hear them.* Costa doesn't lower his head; he holds the attorney's gaze, mumbling, *You piece of shit, you motherfucker.* His jaws are clenched and his lips are white, but I am nine years old and a handsome red knight in tortoiseshell glasses has ridden into the stairwell, a tall avenger bedecked with ermine, Saint George with his long lance, so you can spit all the venom you want, you demon.

The prosecuting attorney itemizes the facts, victim by victim. I am second in the recitation; he seizes the photo of me as a little girl, printed on A4 paper, with my timid smile, my round-necked T-shirt and my freckles, and he brandishes me at Costa. *Do you remember this little girl? This little girl whom you raped!* Costa leaps up, his fist raised, his face purple and swollen, bulging with hate. *You're the one who raped that child, you cocksucker!* he screams, *You're the child-rapist, motherfucker!* And even though I am nothing but pure terror huddled on a bench, this violence, I recognize it, I know it by heart, it is what has mutilated me all these years, this ugliness, I can finally see it outside myself, released, and I sit up straight. The burning tears evaporate as they roll down my cheeks.

The judge tells Costa to be quiet and he sits back down, but no sooner has the prosecuting attorney begun speaking about Marguerite, who sits beside me, trembling and dignified, her fingers interlaced with mine, he starts ranting again, spitting and cursing, and when it's Clara's turn, *It's all lies! I was in Germany, in Dusseldorf! This is scandalous; I'm going to tell the press! Motherfucker!* The guards seize him and drag him toward the exit, still screaming.

We are dealing with someone addicted to violence; there can be no doubt of recidivism. For all these lives destroyed, I ask the court for a twenty-year prison term, the maximum sentence allowed by the law.

That night I go to a concert. I sing at the top of my lungs; I dance; I drink caipirinhas. The music fills me, moves me. I dance; I am immense and infinite, I am thrumming and vibrating with life; I repeat a mantra again and again in my head: *it's going to be all right, you'll see*; I chant it ferociously. I hoist it as my flag, embroidering each of my thoughts with it on this last night, dizzy with alcohol and hope.

D ay seven. The final day. Giovanni Costa is there. It's time for the defense attorneys to speak. They aren't Secrétaires de la Conférence for nothing, and since we're in the Victor Hugo courtroom, each of them quotes from *The Last Day of a Condemned Man*. The phrases are beautiful and well-crafted: *A trial is the time for a man's reintegration into society, rather than his banishment from it.* They remind the court that it is judging a human being, not a monster, and argue that *the scales of Justice were unfairly tipped by that empty dock*, the more pugnacious of the two working to unravel the tight mesh of the accusation.

In circuit court, the defendant has the last word. It is an opportunity to speak without anyone being allowed to interrupt, its duration determined by the presiding judge.

Giovanni Costa stands up, and smiles, and addresses the court for the first time. In a jumbled combination of French and Italian that is difficult to understand, he talks about Pétain, wasps, Cardinal Mazarin, real Italian pasta, Garibaldi, the restoration of antique furniture, Mussolini, his life as a housebreaker. He talks without pausing to draw breath, jumping from one idea to the next. He is clearly enjoying himself, and I need him to account for what he did to us. Two of the other victims and I stand up together and face him, hoping to get a reaction out of him, but there is nothing; he doesn't flinch, doesn't look at us, imperturbable, all-powerful. He keeps going, playing his game, rambling, droning his history of France for idiots, and I can't take it anymore; I flee the court-room and run down the wide marble corridor; I run, and my legs give out, and I fall, and I cry, there on my hands and knees, and my tears are black.

Surrounded, lifted up, physically supported by my aunt and my attorney, I pull myself together and slide silently back onto the wooden bench to subject myself to more of his mocking, erratic gibberish, his grand finale.

Whenever the judge orders him to address the facts of the case, he acts outraged. *I don't have it in me to be a sadist or a rapist*, he protests. *We don't rape two- and three-year-old babies in Italy,* or he lists the contents of a suitcase he left in that hotel in Dusseldorf.

And when, after forty interminable minutes, the judge finally requests that he wrap it up, he says solemnly, *Ladies and gentlemen of the jury; Your Honor; pardon me, I tell you with all my heart that I am not a rapist.* We all quiver at that *pardon me*, but for nothing; it's hopeless, just an Italian mannerism, a *prego*, a meaningless word.

With that, the debates are closed. The presiding judge, the assessors, and the jurors retire to deliberate.

During these seven days spent together, I have scruti-nized the faces of the jurors, their features drawn with sym-pathy. A thousand times I have wanted to join them outside to smoke a cigarette on the steps of the Palais, but we have each kept to our places, not venturing across the borders of the law, and now there is nothing left to add. It's up to them to decide.

The hours spent killing time while awaiting a decision are strange ones; I wander the too-elegant streets of central Paris, irresistibly drawn back toward the Palais and its jurors sequestered inside, clutching my phone as if it were a pregnancy test.

What did you do, Giovanni? What did you spend those hours thinking about? Who are you, in the cramped silence of a cell, when no one is watching?

It's time. Sooner than the clerk predicted. Six hours of deliberation for a hundred and seven questions. They didn't waste any time. My father jumps into a taxi; my aunt onto her bike, and a lot of the girls you tried to destroy, Giovanni, rush to converge on the Victor Hugo courtroom, to hear the verdict.

Another hour spent waiting for the defense attorneys, who are unreachable; an hour of going around in circles to pass the time. Finally, the defense team arrives. We all stand. The jurors file in.

Giovanni Costa is found guilty.
On all counts.
He is sentenced to eighteen years in prison.

We fall into each other's arms, beaming wide, shy smiles at one another. I have spent so many days, months, years sitting on this wooden bench, waiting for the pronouncement of my release. Now it's your turn to be locked up, Giovanni. Your turn to bear the full weight of your hatred.

You're standing up, back very straight, your chin high, your eyes like steel marbles, and suddenly your accent has disappeared completely; your diction is clear; your words are surgical in their clarity: *Pardon me, Your Honor; since you are the instigator of my defeat, wipe your own ass with it tonight, in bed with your partner.*

Five days later, I receive a registered letter. Giovanni Costa has appealed the verdict. He did it on his own, without consulting his attorneys, on the evening of the decision, as soon as he arrived at the remand center.

I try not to sink. I tell myself he will not win this one. I sink anyway. I don't have the strength to start all over again. I don't have the strength to wait two or three years for a new trial to be convened in another department, to stay alone in a strange city, to strip myself bare again in front of a new panel of jurors. I have a life to live. It's been waiting for me for so long.

But I will go anyway, and I will encourage all the other victims to come too. Without our trembling testimonies, our breaking voices, our tear-drenched faces, without us, the horror of the crime will be dulled, and the criminal will win. When jurors aren't affected emotionally, they're more indulgent. I will go.

I hoped, naively, that the presiding magistrate would use this trial as an opportunity to advance the rights of victims of sexual violence. I hoped in vain. He knows how our lives were ripped apart; he has listened, testimony after testimony, to accounts of the long-term consequences. He knows that Costa is penniless, that the damages he is sentenced to pay to the plaintiffs *as compensation for the damages sustained* will be symbolic sums. He knows that symbols go some way toward making amends; he knows the power of his long, ermine-trimmed red robe; he knows the impact of his words. But he sticks to the old jurisprudence; he adheres to the existing penalties: fifteen thousand euros for rape, seven thousand for sexual assault. In France, you can destroy a woman's life for the price of a used car.

To one of us, whose story is no more or less terrifying, no more or less sordid, he awards double. Why? We don't know. There isn't necessarily any rhyme or reason to these decisions. Did he find her story more touching? Worthier of the State's consideration? Is her life worth more? Suffering isn't enough; we have to deserve the empathy we receive.

We all appeal his decisions, except her. He has succeeded in creating a breach between us.

This morning, on a public radio station, a comedian added *an uncle who was a little too insistent* to a list of first sexual experiences. Ha ha ha. I turn off the radio. When will people stop confusing sexuality with violence, sexual desire with an addiction to stress, consent with being in a state of shock? What that niece or nephew experienced wasn't sexuality; it was hatred, omnipotence, ugliness. It had nothing to do with pleasure or embracing or caresses, nothing; nothing at all to do with the merging of two bodies.

EPILOGUE

Your body is cold. You died on that day, that sunny day in May, and there is nothing I can do to bring you back. Sentence by sentence, I thought writing would allow me to find you again, to save you, and that a kiss on your forehead would be enough to wake you up. But your face is blue, and I don't know how to revive you. So I'm just going to talk to you, the way you used to talk to Grandpa under the plum tree. All these years, you waited for me; you knew that as I made my way toward you, I would find myself. This book is yours. These paper flowers are your crown.

The evil he inflicted on you is inside me; I can't loosen it. It's like a granite boulder in the middle of a prairie. But now I know it's there; now I remember, and I play, and romp, and whoop with my son until we collapse, exhausted from tickling and laughing, in the wild grass, and nothing is further away from me than those images of the past. Sometimes I wrap my arms around the man I love, and our bodies thrill with joy, and nothing exists in us but the joy of being alive.

Life never relents. In the deepest depths of the oceans, in the shadows, it gleams.

In my mouth, my throat, I feel the explosive sweetness of biting into a crisp apple. I feel, in my nostrils and all through my windpipe, the scent of pine needles rolled between my fingertips, the vibrant moistness of a handful of damp soil against my palm.

Although I have changed the names of the other victims in this book, they have been with me through every step of the writing process, and it is they who gave me the courage to keep going.

Thank you to Muriel Salmona, my doctor of botany and underwater archaeology.

Thank you to my attorney, Agnès Cittadini, for her passion, her skill, and her humanity.

Thank you to my family and friends, to everyone who gave me their trust, their tenderness, their humor, and their love.

ABOUT THE AUTHOR

Adélaïde Bon is a French writer, actress and voice artist. She is a graduate of the École Supérieure d'Art Dramatique in Paris, and she has acted in state theaters and for television, as well as devised and performed in numerous shows in factories, trains, museums, and conferences. In parallel, she completed five years of training on issues of gender equality under the auspices of a feminist company partnered with the European Association Against Violence Against Women and the Mémoire Traumatique Association led by Dr. Muriel Salmona. She lives in Paris. *The Little Girl on the Ice Floe* is her first book.